MW00624868

F

THE SEVEN STAGES OF THE SOUL

"This important book represents the distillation of a lifetime's reading, reflection and experience in providing wise guidance for discerning readers who are looking for a more profound understanding of the meaning of our spiritual journey in life. Written in a simple and accessible style, Joe's book provides frameworks and approaches that enable us to see the deeper patterns in our close relationships and the underlying significance of our intentions as life presents us with just those situations best suited to our stage of learning and unfoldment. An illuminating and insightful read."

—David Lorimer,
Programme Director, Scientific
and Medical Network (SMN)
and Editor of *Paradigm Explorer*

"The authenticity and integrity of Seven Steps is grounded in the author's own life-long and soul-long journey of inner and outer discovery. In revealing a quest that whilst unique to everyone, yet common to all, the book is a beautifully clear, practical, compassionate and wise companion. As 'spiritual beings having a human experience' it offers a map of the territory we all traverse; offering a guiding light, step by step, of our way towards the eventual home-coming of our soul."

—Dr Jude Currivan, Cosmologist,
Co-founder of "WholeWorld-View"
and Author of *The Cosmic Hologram*

"Seventh heaven awaits those who read and heed Joe St. Clair's latest book *The Seven Stages of The Soul*. It is a marvellous masterful integration of powerful time-honoured spiritual wisdom that nourishes the soul with a feast of information in its quest to find truth. This wonderful book is truly unique, unlike any other I have read on the subject. It offers a fresh approach to enlightenment in clear, concise and practical language, making it an invaluable resource for seekers aspiring to successfully navigate the path to divine illumination. I highly recommend it."

—John R. Audette, MS,
President & CEO, Eternea, Inc.
Founder, International Association
for Near-Death Studies, Inc.

"A refreshing and informative book that cuts right to the heart of spirituality by exploring the soul-path we all have to undertake. Essential reading for those interested in living a more purposeful and fulfilling life as well as an enjoyable and stimulating read full of wisdom and insight."

—Giles Hutchins, Adviser, Speaker,
Chair of "The Future Fit Leadership Academy"
and Author of *The Illusion of Separation*

THE SEVEN STAGES
OF THE SOUL

THE SEVEN STAGES OF THE SOUL

The ultimate guide for all souls on the journey of life

JOE ST CLAIR

PECORARO
SULLIVAN
PUBLISHING COMPANY

This book is dedicated to
all the beautiful souls and Lightworkers
that I have met on my journey through life
and whom I continue to meet every day.
Thank you for sharing your wisdom,
your humility and your friendship.
Without you this book would not have
been possible and I am eternally
indebted to you.

Copyright © 2020 by Joe St Clair
Pecoraro Sullivan Publishing Company

All rights reserved. No part of this publication may be
used or reproduced in any form or by any means,
electronic or mechanical without written permission
from the publisher, except in the case of brief quotations
embodied in critical articles and reviews.

Library of Congress Cataloging-in-Publication Data
St Clair, Joe
The Seven Stages of The Soul
1. New Age 2. Spirituality
ISBN: 978-1-8381666-0-1 (paperback)
ISBN: 978-1-8381666-1-8 (hardcover)
ISBN: 978-1-8381666-2-5 (ePub)

Pecoraro Sullivan Publishing Company
P. O. Box 7892, General Post Office, Hong Kong

www.PSpub.Co

INDEX

Introduction.. xi
Prologue xiv
The Language of the Soul's Journey.................. xxi
The Nature of the Soul xxv

PART ONE

The Journey of the Soul 31
The Hero's Journey 33
The Tarot 37
The Chakras... 43
Navigating your Soul Journey................................ 47
Relationships in the Spiritual Context................. 57
The Ladder to the Stars 65
Many Precious Lives 69
The Soul's Journey from
the Earth Plane to the Spiritual Plane 75
The Taming of the Ego 91
The Law of Karma... 105
The Law of Intention 115
Looking into the Mirror 121
Vibrations, Frequencies and Energies 123

PART TWO

The Soul's Journey on the Earth Plane
(The Seven Stages)... 129
Stage One... 137
Stage Two 157
Stage Three... 167
Stage Four... 177
Stage Five... 189
Stage Six 199
Stage Seven 213

Appendix One - Identifying Souls on
Different Levels... 238
Appendix Two - Applying the Wisdom
of the Seven Stages of the Soul 241
Appendix Three - Spiritual Crisis in Context 245

Afterword 247
About the Author... 259
Recommended Reading.. 251
References... 253

Introduction

As human beings, sharing the same biology and conscious awareness, there comes a time in our life when most, if not all of us, pause and reflect on the big questions that have been asked from time immemorial: "What is the purpose of my life?", "What am I here for?", "Who am I?" and "What is the nature of reality?". Although the questions may differ slightly from individual to individual, the underlying quest for wisdom, truth and meaning are virtually identical. The goal of this book is to provide a useful guidebook or route map for everyone who is seeking answers to these deep and important questions by sharing many universal truths and insights into what makes us not just unique human beings, but also beautiful souls.

The book is in two parts. The first half of the book (Part One) is about the nature of the life we live today and examines the distinctions and characteristics of the two different worlds or realities that we inhabit - the mundane world of everyday reality that is our 'normality' as human beings living on planet Earth - as well as the workings of the more esoteric hidden parallel world of 'Spirit'. The information in the first half of the book has been drawn from many sources as well as personal first hand experience and is fully referenced accordingly.

The second half of the book (Part Two) is mostly unreferenced and deliberately so. The content and information contained within Part Two was delivered to me in a single 'spiritual download' during August 2019 and I can claim no credit for the wisdom it imparts. I was merely the chosen 'vessel' that has transcribed the information imparted to me into the best words I could find. The information I received was unknown to me before this download and I can only humbly thank the spiritual world for allowing me the privilege and the honour of being the chosen recipient of this very important wealth of information and insights.

The spirit world has made it clear that they wish this knowledge to be disseminated far and wide because of their concerns for the future of our fragile planet and for the future prospects for ourselves, our children and our grandchildren.

I see this book therefore, as a small but important contribution to the growing global conscious awakening of thousands of enlightened souls embarking on a personal journey of spiritual awakening. A new paradigm and a new world view are slowly emerging from a dysfunctional, patriarchal and egotistical period of human history and this awakening is essential to rebalance male and female energies and to herald a new era where materiality and ego-based greed gives way to a new way of viewing our planet based on connectedness, compassion and unity consciousness. Indeed, this global spiritual awakening is long overdue and may well be the prime catalyst that is needed to bring our fragile planet back from the brink before it is too late.

Throughout the book there are references to many concepts that may be new to readers or outside of their normal experience or current belief system even though these concepts have been around for many thousands of years. I make no apology for this. It is not the purpose of this book to prove or justify any of the material presented here for two reasons. Firstly, any attempt to try and unequivocally prove the validity of the material would require a book twice the size in length and would miss the objective of the book. Secondly, there are many other excellent books available which serve to provide detailed and credible scientific or other forms of proof should readers want to investigate these topics in more depth. At the end of this book the 'Recommended Reading' section gives a list of such books.

Joe St Clair
May 2020

Prologue

It was Lao Tzu, the Chinese philosopher and founder of Taoism, who famously said, "Every journey starts with the first step" and that is true for every one of us on this beautiful, magical journey we call 'Life'. But what is life? And why does it sometimes have to be such a tough journey? Why do we have to endure such heartache, grief, distress, loss, frustration and hardship along with joy, friendship, happiness, fulfilment and love? These questions have been asked by mankind since the beginning of human existence and we, as a species, have often looked to the great sages, shamans, wise elders, gurus and spiritual leaders to make sense of the world and give us the answers. Sometimes, the answers have been given through the filters of an established religion where a consensus answer has been formulated to appease the masses. Many individuals, however, have sought their own answers to these perennial deep questions through psychics, mediums and other gentle souls who have been privileged to see 'through the veil' into the spirit world or have made contact with the spirit world directly.

At the heart of almost all religions there is a belief in some kind of afterlife which is seen as the reward for all souls who have diligently followed their chosen path, faced up to their daily challenges as a human being and are now ready to face the last and greatest challenge of all, which we call 'death' but can be more accurately termed 'transition'. Every single one of us has our own unique story and it is the story of our life. But where does this life really begin? And where does it end?

All journeys must start at the beginning, and, just as a traditional fairy story starts with 'Once upon a time' - this is probably the best phrase to start our examination of our own soul's journey on the long path to enlightenment, wisdom and ultimate fulfilment.

Once upon a time...there was a beautiful soul conceived by the brightest light in the universe that we might choose to call our first 'Mother'. It was a soul perfect in every way. Untarnished, innocent, pure and glowing with a perpetually glowing inner light that expresses itself and manifests itself with wonder, hope, joy and most of all love. Unconditional love.

And that soul is you.

Stop for a moment and breathe deeply. It is time to openly accept that you are a unique and very special beautiful and much-loved eternal soul. You are a soul blessed with immortality and gifted with an eternal inner 'passport' to be used both for your brief sojourn on planet Earth and to gain entry into the spiritual realms after transition.

Your journey through this vast universe and through both the unseen and the visible worlds is a never-ending adventure that you have been blessed to experience. It is an honour and a privilege that you should never underestimate. The universe has granted you the most precious gift it is possible to give. And that gift is life. From a small seed bursting with an as-yet unmanifest potential the universe has breathed the magic of life into the heart of the seed that has become you. And the seed has then flourished and become a unique soul that is eternally beautiful and immortal and has sought a temporary dwelling place to manifest itself and sought the perfect location to manifest its inherent potential. A potential about to be realised.

As Doctor Brenda Davis explains:

"In the beginning there was only the Source, which wished to experience the material world. Out of itself, it created a myriad of souls which were released into the cosmos. Those fledgling souls experienced the universe, learned and developed and returned to the soul planes, perhaps briefly for hundreds of years, before venturing out once more in order to evolve further. Each of us is one of those souls, still journeying, still on our evolutionary path. We have ascended through various life forms to humanity and we are still growing, still striving towards our goal of enlightenment".
("Journey of the Soul" by Dr. Brenda Davies)

The soul's choice of a dwelling place is inside you. Inside your physical present body. And the soul's choice of location is on a small blue speck in the vastness of the universe that we call planet Earth. You are that unique soul bursting with life and opportunity and your testing ground is the Earth that you stand upon. In many ways it can be likened to a school because it is somewhere that you need to attend in order to learn. It is the lessons that we learn during our time at 'Earth school' that will determine how we progress on our journey through each incarnation. Earth school is not always a bed of roses though. It can also be a school of 'hard knocks' where you sometimes need to stand your ground against the odds and at other times be humble enough to accept the wisdom imparted by others who are wiser than you. Are you now ready to take that momentous first step on the road to fulfilment, enlightenment, peace, love and understanding?

The soul's path is not, of course, a literal path, but rather a metaphorical path. Our journey through life never follows a literal path - but the path is still the perfect metaphor for our experience of being alive and traversing all life's obstacles, challenges and temptations.

This idea or concept of a journey from life to death is familiar in all cultures throughout history and almost every story, myth, fable or wisdom-teaching is related directly to this extraordinary journey. In the same way that Joseph Campbell's 'Hero' takes the 'Hero's Journey' as a quest that mirrors our own life journey, or the 'Aspirant' (The Fool) that experiences every step through the Tarot's Major Arcana, these stories reflect our own personal quest to find the 'treasure' at the end of the path, like the gold at the end of the rainbow. But, in this case, the treasure is not the riches sought through greed and desire but the far greater rewards of wisdom and truth.

But, before we start on our quest to fully understand the 'Soul's Journey', there are a few very important terms or words that need to be clarified right at the outset in order to avoid any misunderstanding or confusion. These words are key to our understanding of the workings of the spiritual world that we shall be visiting and examining over the following pages so we need to be very clear on their meanings.

The Language of
the Soul's Journey

The term *'Earth Plane'* refers to our existence here on planet Earth and in essence is referring to what we consider to be our everyday reality. It is our normality and refers to our daily lives and day to day routines and challenges.

In contrast, the term *'Spirit World'* or *'Spiritual Realms'* (which can be used interchangeably) refers to the parallel world of spirit where we came from originally and where we return to after each of our many lives (i.e. after Transition or Death). In some contexts, I have chosen to substitute the word *'Universe'* for 'spirit world' simply because many people use this term when they receive messages from the 'other side'. So, messages from the spirit world or the universe are essentially the same thing.

The term *'Source'* refers to the creator of the Universe and all things (I prefer not to use any words with religious connotations). 'Source' is the creator of all souls and can be best visualised as the brightest light in the universe from which everything else emanates. After our final life in the material realm of physicality we all, ultimately, return to the same Source from which we originally came.

Throughout this book I will substitute the word *'Transition'* for 'Death' because in the context of this book there is no death. There is just transition from our earthly existence to our spiritual existence between lives. The soul is immortal and physical death of the body does not have any bearing on the immortal nature of the soul. The word transition is also used in another context within this book when referring to the transition from one soul 'Stage' to the next soul stage.

The words *'Soul Group'* and *'Soul Contract'* are explained in more detail in Part One but in simple terms our Soul Group refers to a group of around 20-30 souls that we interact with regularly over many different incarnations (lives). Our 'Soul Contract' is an agreement that we made with our spiritual guides before this current incarnation which defines the list of 'tasks' and the list of 'challenges' that we agreed to undertake within this current incarnation. This contract also includes the people we need to meet and interact with and the lessons we need to learn on our soul journey. It can also be expressed as our *'Life Purpose'*.

The term *'Guardian Angel'* refers to a spirit guide that resides in the spiritual world and is our primary guide throughout all of our lifetimes. Our guide can be male, female or androgynous and has always been with us since our soul was first created. Our spirit guide is always with us and is always watching over us and caring for us from birth to transition. Our spirit guide rarely intervenes directly into our lives but can choose to do so at times of emotional crisis or when we are in danger. Usually our spirit guide is the first to greet us when we transition. (Note that the term 'Angel' is a label some people have chosen to give to this spiritual entity but is not to be confused with the Christian type of 'Angel' as depicted in religion, literature and art. A better term would be 'Primary Guide' but 'Guardian Angel' is used in this book because this is the term most people are familiar with).

Our *'Spirit Guides'* are other guides that support us both on the Earth Plane and within the spiritual realms but are secondary to the predominance of our own 'Guardian Angel' who has prime responsibility for our spiritual growth. When we are between lives and temporarily residing in the spiritual realms, the guides act as 'teachers' or 'mentors' and interact with us directly. When we are living on the 'Earth Plane' these guides are invisible to us but can act as intermediaries if, for example, we desire contact with our departed loved ones via a medium or psychic or if we seek guidance whilst in deep meditation about a spiritual matter.

Our *'Soul Mate'* is our primary partner, but not always the *only* partner, that we have incarnated with during many lifetimes and with whom we have the closest affinity.

'Twin Flames' are like a human twin that we share our spiritual journey with through many incarnations providing a balance between the masculine and the feminine aspects of our personality. We are always intimately connected to our Twin Flame but not as emotionally attached as we are with our 'Soul Mate' with whom we share intimacy. Having one's twin flame as a soul mate happens occasionally but is a rare occurrence.

'Karma' is the sum of all the accumulated experiences we have gathered throughout all of our lifetimes and is thus a unique and eternal record of the consequences of all the intentions and actions we have ever undertaken. It is sometimes referred to as our 'Akashic Record'.

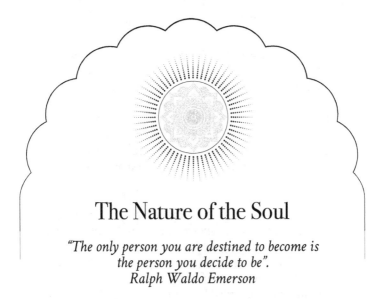

The Nature of the Soul

"The only person you are destined to become is the person you decide to be".
Ralph Waldo Emerson

The word used most frequently in this book is probably the word 'Soul' and for this reason this word needs a little more attention and explanation than the other related words defined above. It would be wrong to start on our journey through the pages ahead without first being very clear on what is meant by 'soul' so that there can be no misunderstanding. So let's start right at the beginning and get to know the soul that is at the heart of every single one of us - the essence of everything we have ever been, everything we are today and everything we will ever be in the future.

Throughout history there have been countless different meanings attached to the word 'soul' and in many religions and belief systems other words and pictures are used in place of the word 'soul' - but where the central concept remains much the same. There have always been - and probably always will be - sceptics, rationalists and disbelievers to whom the very idea of a 'soul' is just nonsense. And there are still many hard-nosed scientists and 'rationalists' around who deny the existence of a soul on the grounds of 'no scientific evidence' despite the ever increasing body of other forms of evidence and literature on the subject.

But to put these contrasting views into some sort of perspective it is helpful to relate them to the timeline of mankind's existence on Earth. As Robert E. Cox states in his excellently researched book:

"Modern physical science has persisted for a few hundred years and provided the basis for one of the most rapidly changing and turbulent periods in human history. By contrast, the ancient spiritual science persisted for thousands of years and served as the basis for some of the most stable and enduring civilizations the world has ever known".
("Creating the Soul Body" by Robert E. Cox)

In early Greek philosophy the soul was equated with what they called the "breath of life" and was recognised as being both the source of all life as well as the agent that enabled the prime forces of the universe to manifest. In Latin the word 'anima' and the Greek word 'psyche' both come from the same semantic root word meaning 'breath' and it was believed that this breath of life enabled the physical body to function until the point of death when the breath of life would simply leave the body rather than being extinguished. This all-pervading breath was also viewed as the source of all life which contained within itself an inherent wisdom in the form of 'knowing' and was spread across the whole universe as the underlying creative force from which all matter derived. This concept of the universe being a connected 'one-ness' that unites both macrocosm and microcosm, in which the individual immortal soul is an integral part of the whole universe, is what Plato referred to as the 'anima mundi' or 'world soul'.

In very recent times the borders between science and spirituality have been crumbling and an increasing number of scientists are now becoming more open minded to the notion of the existence of some form of a soul. Some of the recent discoveries in quantum physics and the behaviours of sub-atomic particles in particular are changing our views about what constitutes 'reality' and descriptions of the quantum field are extraordinarily similar to a number of ancient mythologies relating to spiritual concepts and the nature of the soul.

Many scientists that we expect to be hardcore materialists are, in fact, quite the opposite. Max Planck, one of the founders of quantum physics said, *"Spirit is the original basis of all matter, reality and true existence"*. And Albert Einstein stated that, *"Everyone who is seriously involved in the pursuit of science becomes convinced that a Spirit is manifest in the laws of the universe"*.

Living in an increasingly technology driven, materialist, scientific, consumerist, rationalist, methodical and antiseptically sanitised world, it is easy for us to lose sight of the magic and wonder of the wider universe. It is easy for us to become disconnected from who we really are and from the inner intelligence that we were seeded from. To be re-connected with the vital spark that is our true self - an immortal beautiful and unique soul, is our birthright and our privilege. It is time to reclaim our right to be who we truly are.

PART ONE

*"Strange as it may seem
there are even men among us
who think that the soul dies with the body.
Mankind are great fools
and will believe anything".
Erasmus 1519*

The Journey of the Soul

*"A stairway to the sky is set up for me
that I may ascend on it to the sky".*
Egyptian Pyramid Text c.2400 BCE

For all souls on 'the path' the journey from start to finish is more of an arduous expedition than a gentle stroll. It is a path we all have to follow whether we choose to or not and while some of us approach it as an exciting adventure, for others it can be a torturous ordeal. To make progress requires overcoming a series of very difficult challenges and obstacles which test us to the extreme and, because we all are all individuals, the way that we cope with these challenges can be markedly different.

When we are consciously *aware* that we are on a soul journey we are better enabled to cope with the stresses of the journey because we understand our role in the bigger picture. But for the millions of souls who have little, or no, conscious awareness that they are on a soul path or soul journey the experience can be disconcerting, frightening or even terrifying. Similarly, for many souls, the transition from one 'stage' to the next 'higher stage' on their journey can be a cause for celebration and reward but for souls who are not aware of this process, the shift from one stage to another can sometimes cause them massive confusion, anxiety and stress.

This book is dedicated to helping everyone on their path or soul journey whatever stage or level they have reached. This book also attempts to explain the process in detail in order to bring clarity and structure - and, of course, to help every beautiful soul on their unique and wonderful journey.

Let the journey begin...

The Hero's Journey

The 'Journey of the Soul' on the soul's path from ignorance to maturity or innocence to enlightenment is not a new story. In fact, it really is the oldest story in the world and almost every nation and every culture in the world throughout recorded time has myths, legends and stories that are a reflection of the timeless journey of the soul. There may be subtle nuances that are culturally different and different metaphors may be used to explain different concepts - but essentially the story retains the same framework. It is an adventure story where the protagonist or hero of the story undertakes a difficult quest.

The quest involves many hardships, challenges, obstacles or the completion of many tasks. And the hero has to overcome all of these hurdles in order to find the treasure, whatever that treasure might be, so he or she can return home triumphantly with the prize. Almost every film in the world follows this same broad plot line from 'The Wizard of Oz' to the 'Star Wars' chronicles or from Disney's 'Pinocchio' or 'The Lion King' to 'Harry Potter'. Indeed the most famous films ever made can all be boiled down to having the same central themes running through them. But even in the days before film was invented, the stories our ancestors told around campfires, of great mythical heroes or classical epics like 'Jason and the Golden Fleece' or 'The Labours of Hercules' served to impart the same truths and wisdom through the medium of storytelling.

The famous cultural historian, Joseph Campbell, studied myths and legends for many years before publishing his seminal work, "The Hero with a Thousand Faces", which is now an international bestseller and a recognised classic that examines in detail the origins and the structures of all the world's greatest stories.

Whatever the myth, legend or fairy tale might be called - and in whatever age of history the story is set in - the 'structure' of the story always remains virtually the same. The metaphor always reflects the journey of the immortal soul's journey from ignorance to enlightenment and the quest for justice and truth. The name of the hero or heroine might change and the location of the adventure might change, but the essential plotline is constant. It is the timeless tale of an innocent soul traversing the challenges of life on the Earth Plane in order to acquire enough wisdom to transcend the so-called 'human condition' and ultimately ascend to the place of eternal bliss. The ultimate goal of the soul's journey, therefore, is to return to where it originated from - the Source - so that the circle of life can be completed. This is a sort of homecoming and indeed, the prime goal of every soul is simply to return 'Home' after having finally located the ultimate treasure - wisdom!

According to Joseph Campbell:

"Only birth can conquer death - the birth, not of the old thing again, but of something new. Within the

soul, within the body social, there must be - if we are to experience long survival – a continuous 'recurrence of birth' to nullify the unremitting recurrences of death".
("The Hero With A Thousand Faces" by Joseph Campbell)

Throughout this book, the Journey of the Soul that we will be exploring in depth, will be using Joseph Campbell's book, "The Hero with a Thousand Faces" as its guidebook, framework and 'blueprint' so that we can contextualise the key elements of the soul's journey that we are all traversing right at this very moment.

But Joseph Campbell's book is not the only guidebook that we can turn to in order to make sense of our own soul journey through this current life. There is another very ancient and much revered source of wisdom and knowledge that we can also use to help us and guide us on our personal journey. It is called the 'Tarot' - a pack of sacred cards that has been used for centuries to tell people the story of the journey of the soul - picture images that have been used to beautifully explain the soul's path on its journey through life - long before the advent of the written word.

In addition to the Hero's Journey and the Tarot, there is another third element that we can also turn to for guidance and to give structure to our quest and these are the seven 'Chakras'. For just as we move through seven stages or levels of experience on our soul journey, we are also powered by the energy delivered to our bodies through the seven major chakra points. And, as we ascend the 'ladder' towards immortality we also ascend through the chakras from the first 'Root' chakra at the start of our journey to the 'Crown' chakra that will ultimately reconnect us to Source.

Together these three strands of wisdom can help us tune into the inner unseen world of spirit and thereby learn how to navigate our way through both our earthbound human life and also the onward journey of our soul as it traverses the spiritual realms.

So before we embark on our quest let's first get acquainted with our guides on the journey. Let's now take a closer look at the Tarot.

The Tarot

Just as our soul journey can be compared to Joseph Campbell's Hero's Journey in global mythology, there is another useful analogy or framework that we can also use to help understand the significance of this incredible and timeless journey and it is called the Tarot.

The Tarot is set of mysterious and magical images that have been converted over time into a set of playing cards that are distantly related to a set of modern traditional playing cards with four 'Suits' and a 'Joker'. There are many theories and legends attached to the Tarot because of its powerful symbolism and ability to give card users deep insights and intuitions when concentrating on the images. No-one has yet discovered the true origins of the Tarot and opinions differ as to where the earliest packs were created. China, India and Persia are all contenders but there are also images that can be traced back to the ancient Celts, Morocco and medieval Italy. In his excellent book on the Tarot, Richard Cavendish also observed that:

"The imagery of the Tarot has been traced to the collective unconscious, or to the symbolism of Dante's 'Divine Comedy'. The name Tarot itself has been derived from Egyptian, Hebrew or Latin. The older

cards are very beautiful and have an air of profound significance. They tug at half-buried memories and obscure connections associated with mythology, legend, magic and folk belief".
("The Tarot" by Richard Cavendish)

The standard Tarot pack has four 'suits': Swords, Cups, Coins (or Pentacles) and Batons (or Sceptres/ Wands) and these correspond respectively to todays' suits of Spades, Hearts, Diamonds and Clubs. But the main difference between the Tarot pack and the modern pack is that the Tarot has another 22 cards which have their own names and numbers. These 22 cards are known as the 'Major Arcana' and all the other cards are known as the 'Minor Arcana'(i.e. the four suits). The only card that has survived the passage of time from the ancient Tarot to the current playing card is the 'Joker' card but the original name for the 'Joker' was 'The Fool'.

The purpose of this book is not to explain the history or depth of wisdom embodied in the Tarot but merely to use some of the Major Arcana cards as 'signposts' on our soul's journey. The reason for this is very simple. The twenty-two cards of the Major Arcana tell a story through the powerful imagery of the Tarot cards and that journey closely aligns to Joseph Campbell's Hero's Journey - except in the case of the Tarot, this becomes "The Journey of The Fool".

So, whether we choose to use the Hero's Journey, or the Journey of The Fool as our framework for understanding our own personal soul journey it does not matter. Both stories are of equal relevance because both, at a deeper level, tell exactly the same story - the story of a soul's journey from birth to transition and ignorance to enlightenment.

The 22 cards that compose the Tarot's 'Major Arcana' are as follows:

Card 0 The Fool or 'Aspirant'
Card 1 The Magician (or Juggler)
Card 2 The High Priestess (or Female Pope)
Card 3 The Empress
Card 4 The Emperor
Card 5 The Hierophant
Card 6 The Lovers
Card 7 The Chariot
Card 8 Strength
Card 9 The Hermit
Card 10 The Wheel of Fortune
Card 11 Justice
Card 12 The Hanged Man
Card 13 Death
Card 14 Temperance
Card 15 The Devil
Card 16 The Tower
Card 17 The Star
Card 18 The Moon
Card 19 The Sun
Card 20 Judgement
Card 21 The World

The Journey of The Fool is a journey on many levels and that is the wonder and beauty of the Tarot. It is never a static tool for imparting wisdom but rather a fluid tool that can be used for a wide variety of purposes. It is said that whoever is holding the cards in order to receive knowledge (known in Tarot terminology as the 'Querent') is the one who determines the messages revealed. In other words, Tarot cards have survived the test of time and have evolved as we, as a species, have evolved. By some means, which we may never understand, the Tarot delivers different messages to each of us from an unknown, unseen source.

But, however the Tarot 'works', the key thing to understand is that it does work - and that is the reason it is revered across the world in cultures thousands of miles apart.

Carl Jung, the famous psychoanalyst, studied the Tarot for many years and suggested that the Tarot works because it links us directly to what he called the 'collective unconscious' and that the images on the cards were expressions of 'archetypes' - in other words, images that all cultures instinctively and intuitively recognise because of deeply embedded memories from past lives. This is the magic of the cards. When we hold a card in our hand and let the card 'speak' to our subconscious through the image imprinted on the card, we receive important messages, or guidance which help us to understand deep truths, insights and answers to our unvoiced questions.

It is important in the context of this book to understand that the Tarot, which effectively represents the 'Journey of The Fool', does not mean 'fool' in today's modern sense of the word (i.e. someone who is 'foolish'). This distinction was used to great effect in the works of William Shakespeare. In his masterpiece of literature, 'King Lear', for example, the king's constant companion throughout the play is the 'Fool', who is ostensibly there to provide amusement for the king. But in reality, as the king starts making bad decisions and starts losing his sanity, it is the Fool who starts speaking truth from a place of wisdom.

Similarly, in Tarot terminology, 'The Fool' is not just the simpleton depicted on the cards. Instead the picture represents you and I and indeed all of us who innocently start out on our soul's journey into the unknown, being naïve and unenlightened, and who ultimately return from that journey having gained wisdom and truth.

The Chakras

Just as there are seven stages of our soul's journey whist on the 'Earth Plane' there are also seven chakras or energy centres within our human body. Although not formally recognised yet by mainstream western medicine the existence of the chakras have been known to eastern medicine for centuries.

At the core of our body these seven wheel-like energy points are in a constant state of spin. They are in essence swirling vortices of 'life energy' but with differing properties or characteristics that connect mind, body and spirit together to form an integrated system that maintains our overall health, wellbeing and vitality.

According to Anodea Judith Ph.D. who has spent her life exploring the chakras:

"The chakras are the master programs that govern our life, loves, learning and illumination. As seven vibratory modalities, the chakras form a mythical 'rainbow bridge' - a connecting channel linking Heaven and Earth, mind and body, spirit and matter, past and future".
("Wheels of Life" by Anodea Judith)

The body is the vessel that connects us to consciousness while we live on the Earth Plane and the vessel is powered by the chakras that provide the energy we need to enable us to travel on our life's journey. If we were to liken our body to a car then the chakras would be all the mechanical parts - including the engine and the fuel - that makes the car operate as it should. The soul would be the 'driver' and the ego would be the annoying 'passenger' that keeps trying to take the wheel and take over the driving. More about the ego later.

In a modern world that has been hoodwinked into believing Cartesian and Newtonian notions of a world composed of isolated and separate mechanical parts that only work when physically connected together, the chakra system is an anathema. But in the real world of constant energetic interaction, co-operation and connectedness, the chakras are the perfect metaphor for how the whole is more than just the sum of its parts. Just as the universe, the planets, the Earth, air, water, rocks, minerals, nature and mankind are intrinsically bound together into one holistic unity by one integrated quantum energy field, so it is with the chakras. Although each of the seven chakras has its own unique properties and qualities, they spin together in a synchronised 'energy dance' that serves to keep us, and our energy fields, healthy and fully operational.

Sometimes, one or more of the chakras can be damaged by certain situations and circumstances. It can start to spin or vibrate more slowly and be less efficient which manifests in the physical body as illness. But in most cases, with the right care and attention, the damaged chakra can be repaired and brought back into full spin (though 'vibration' is actually a more exact term than 'spin').

To fully understand the whole chakra system would take another book in its own right and it is not the purpose of this book to delve into the mysteries and intricacies of the chakra system. The seven chakras are merely used as a framework that provide another way of understanding our soul's journey on the Earth Plane.

This book describes how each individual soul navigates its own path from starting out as a young, immature or 'baby' soul at 'Level One' of its journey, through seven stages of soul development until it finally arrives at 'Level Seven' having achieved 'soul maturity'. So, in effect, each Stage of spiritual development can be equated with a specific chakra that manifests different 'qualities'. For example, the first chakra known as the root chakra, which lies at the base of the spine, has always been recognised as having the qualities of connection to the physical body, the ego, the tangible and the material. By way of contrast, the seventh or 'crown' chakra manifests the qualities of unity consciousness, liberation, serenity and bliss. These qualities, which have been recognised for many centuries, perfectly align with the qualities manifested at the equivalent stages of the soul and hence are another perfect metaphor for our individual spiritual journeys.

This journey can be paralleled with advanced yoga practitioners who use each of the seven chakras in turn to raise their overall level of health and spiritual awareness through the medium of the 'Kundalini' (In Hinduism the kundalini is visualised as a coiled serpent that rests at the root or base chakra until awakened. Once awakened, the serpent rises up slowly through the seven chakra points of the body via the spinal cord, finally arriving at the seventh crown chakra where it reaches enlightenment).

Together the Hero's Journey, as described by Joseph Campbell, the Journey of the Fool in Tarot mythology and the seven chakras of Hindu and Buddhist philosophy, all combine to give us the perfect framework to help us better understand the mysteries of our own personal journey on this planet as immortal souls. They will serve as our three guides as we explore the wonder and the intricacies of the amazing journey that every single one of us is following right at this very moment.

Navigating your Soul Journey

"There are more things in heaven and earth, Horatio,
than are dreamt of in your philosophy".
William Shakespeare, Hamlet

This book repeatedly refers to the seven different aspects of soul development on our soul path and interchangeably uses a number of different terms for these aspects including seven 'Steps', 'Stages' or 'Levels'. Because of the way we have been educated by our schools and our parents, we have become accustomed to wanting a structure for everything we do because we like order. We divide the day into twenty-four hours for example and we divide the week into seven days. We understand that books are divided into chapters and cars travel at kilometres or miles per hour. These delineations help us to make sense of the world and ensure a shared understanding of number, order and hierarchy.

But sometimes boundaries can be blurred. For example, we know there are four seasons but sometimes it is hard to define when Spring finishes and Summer starts when it is not connected to a specific date on a calendar. In the real world, as every farmer knows, sometimes Spring comes early and Summer stays too long. Mankind can create a calendar, but nature won't always conform! And this is just the same when trying to describe the unfolding of our individual soul journeys!

The different experiences we encounter on our soul journey can never be clearly delineated into seven specific time slots - whether we call them stages, steps, levels or even 'modes'. The boundaries between each stage will always be blurred and very often it is a slow transition when moving from one stage to another - sometimes over many years. It can only rarely be pinpointed to a fixed point in time and only a few people can honestly say, "Yesterday I was at Stage Three on my soul path and today I'm at Stage Four!" Although this can - and does - happen for some people, it is actually very rare. So, when this book refers to each step of the journey it is mainly for ease of reference as a kind of map or signpost. Just like a real path the journey is continuous and unfolds before us, so don't get too fixated on what stage you believe you are at!

Similarly, when we examine each of the seven steps on the soul path there will be numerous examples of the characteristics that individuals display during each stage. But once again, don't take this too literally. Life is never quite that simple. Some people who are technically at Stage One may well have developed some characteristics displayed by people in Stage Two and visa-versa. The seven steps are undoubtedly a very useful framework for understanding the evolutionary unfolding of our soul journey, but the boundaries are very flexible. Sometimes, in rare cases, there may even be one or two people at Stage One who display the characteristics of someone at Stage Seven and visa-versa. But this is rare and exceptional. Generally, the path is a linear one that we all undertake from start to finish and the seven-step model is therefore the best possible guide for our purposes and to understand the true nature of the path we are all on. It is a journey that teaches us important life-lessons as we learn to overcome all manner of difficult challenges in order to acquire wisdom in the widest sense of the word.

As Kelly Schwegel so eloquently explains in her excellent book, "The Art of Inner Alchemy":

"Life here on Earth is nothing but a big classroom for your soul. Your soul actually ages, just as your body does. It ages from baby, to infant, to young, to mature to old like your body, except your body ages through time and your soul ages through wisdom gained through multiple lifetimes. This includes lifetimes of learning by making mistakes, doing positive things and negative things, laughing, loving, hurting and harming".
("The Art of Inner Alchemy" by Kelly Schwegel)

At this point, I would like to say something about the concept of 'Religion'. Some people consider themselves 'religious' because they like to align themselves with a particular formalised religion and choose to follow the moral codes, tenets and precepts of their chosen religion. All souls have this inherent right to choose their own modes of worship and many find solace and comfort through religious teachings and practices. Equally, all souls need to fully respect this fundamental right for everyone to be free to follow their own 'calling' to whichever religion they choose. Advanced souls accept this as a 'given' and have no prejudices whatsoever against any religion or religious belief, although it is true to say that some souls within Stage One of their development are sometimes critical of certain religions or practices. But these criticisms (voiced or unvoiced) tend to dissipate as they move into the higher stages of their soul evolution.

There are some religious practitioners, however, who believe that they are 'advanced' or higher level souls because of their status within the organised religion they subscribe to and this is actually untrue. Many individuals who have gained positions of power or seniority on the Earth Plane often assume that this means they have achieved the equivalent status in the Spiritual Realm. Although this is sometimes the case, it is not always the case, and it is perfectly possible for a very high-ranking religious leader in the Earthly Realm to still be at Stage One in the Spiritual Realm. The reasons for this seemingly strange paradox will become apparent in the pages that follow.

In the final analysis however, all religions, however orthodox or unorthodox they might be, all lead us to the same place. As the much revered spiritual philosopher Osho says:

"All the religions are agreed upon one point - that real life begins after death. This life is only a rehearsal, not the real drama. So sacrifice everything to get ready for the drama that is going to happen after death".
("Living Dangerously" - Osho)

The other very crucial point is to do with our understanding of the word 'hierarchy' which we tend to use in the military or corporate world to signify the chain of command from top to bottom. Our society is riddled with examples of hierarchical structures that try to pigeon-hole us all into categories. This was particularly so in the days of class structure in the United Kingdom when we all knew our place in society as 'Upper', 'Middle' or 'Lower' class citizens. Unfortunately, this mindset is still rife in all walks of life, so we tend to subconsciously - or even consciously - think in a hierarchical way.

This is very pertinent when discussing the seven stages of our soul journey because, as there is a natural progression from Stage One to Stage Seven, we tend to automatically assume that Stage Two is superior to Stage One and Stage Three is inferior to Stage Four etcetera. However, nothing could be further from the truth.

When you are reading about each of the seven stages it is very easy to make the assumption that as the soul path is a steady progression towards 'Soul Maturity' there is an implication that those people further along the path are more spiritually mature than those at the start of the path. Although there is some truth in this statement, it is very important to understand the spiritual context of this situation rather than be biased by our own Earth Plane viewpoints and prejudices.

In the spiritual realms the words 'Superior' and 'Inferior' are never used. Nor are the words 'Mature' and 'Immature'. These are human constructs and in this context they are irrelevant. In the spirit world every single soul is a very precious and unique part of creation. Every soul has value and every soul is a beautiful manifestation of its original source and its inherent potential. There are no 'good' souls or 'bad' souls. All of us are just souls following our own path. So, the spirit world treats ALL souls with equal respect regardless of where they happen to be on their own unique soul's journey - from beginning to end.

This means that in the spirit world every single soul is exactly where it is supposed to be on the path. Let me state that again, because this is a fundamental principle that underpins everything else in this book.

"Every single soul is exactly where it is supposed to be on the path".

This fundamental principle needs a little more explanation because it is so crucial to our understanding of how the spirit world works...

On the Earth Plane we live in a very competitive and stressful world. Subconsciously we tend to view the people around us - in our families, workplaces and socially - through the eyes of a competitor. We strive for promotions at work to get not just more money, but for recognition and status. We measure ourselves against our peers and make judgements on who is 'moving up' in the world and who is 'moving down'. We compare our houses and our cars. We compare our exam results. We compare each other on the sports field or our intellectual superiority on quiz nights. We can't help it. This attitude is in our veins and it is what we were all taught at school - "Compete to survive", "It's a dog-eat-dog world", "May the best man win" etc.

But in the spiritual realms all of this is totally irrelevant. We are all souls to be nurtured, loved and respected. There is no 'us and them', there is no 'better or worse' and there is no hierarchy. A homeless beggar on the streets and a multi-millionaire are treated equally in the spirit world. And they are equally loved and welcomed on every step of their respective paths.

Every soul is on a journey and they will remain on that journey throughout not just every lifetime but also in the period between lives. In this sense we are actually on two soul journeys throughout our existence. We take many paths during many different lives on the Earth Plane and we also have to follow a very different path when we are between lives on the Spiritual Plane. But even this very simplified description is not completely accurate - because according to our spiritual guides we sometimes need to follow paths on other worlds as well as planet Earth. They explain that this is sometimes necessary because there are some life-lessons that simply cannot be learned here on planet Earth and therefore require a very different experience. The reason that this is important to understand is because every single one of us is *exactly where we are meant to be* on our journey. And there are no exceptions. Whether we are just taking our first exploratory steps at the very beginning of Stage One or completing the last step of Stage Seven - as individuals, we are all exactly where we are supposed to be.

Sometimes this concept can be hard to fathom when we apply human logic to it. There are many people who constantly strive to better themselves for all sorts of reasons. Some of us want more qualifications, some want to attend courses to learn new skills. Some want to earn more and get a promotion. Others want to learn a foreign language, go travelling or to join a commune. We all want different things and that is good because any self-development is to be applauded.

But it can also bring frustrations.

I know for sure that there will be some readers of this book who already know that they are on a spiritual path and are familiar with a lot of concepts in this book. They may have meditated for years and they may be psychics or healers and consider themselves to be spiritually 'enlightened' already. Does this mean they are already at Stage Seven? The answer is 'possibly, but not necessarily'. They might read this book and recognise their characteristics as being lower down the scale than they thought and that might even annoy or frustrate them. But that's just applying Earth Plane subjective logic to the issue - and in the spiritual realm, to put it bluntly, Earth Plane logic is totally irrelevant.

As a spiritual soul we are ALL - every one of us - exactly where we should be and there are no exceptions. There is no shame in being at Stage One when we believe that we should be at Stage Four or Stage Five. It is just how it is. We are all exactly where we are supposed to be and that is perfect. That is how it has to be. In the spiritual realm everyone is equal. All the time. Not *some* of the time. *All* of the time.

The spiritual world tells us to treat our life on Earth as a classroom because that is exactly what it is supposed to be. If we ask any spiritual entity the question, "Why are we here?" the answer is always the same - "To learn". That is why we are here and that is why we are all on our own individual learning paths. No two paths are the same and that is deliberate, because we all need to learn something different during our Earthly incarnation. That is why we are all - always - exactly where we should be. Because until we have learned a specific lesson that we are here to learn, we cannot take the next step on our journey. We are on a path and on a journey that has a purpose. And the purpose is to follow our own unique spiritual path because it will lead us to places where we need to go in order to learn important lessons relevant to us specifically as an individual soul. You and I may be both walking a similar looking path and may even be at the same stage of development, but the lessons we need to learn may be totally different because of our karma and because of our Soul Contract.

As Ainslie MacLeod explains in his book "The Instruction - living the life your soul intended":

"The soul's purpose is to evolve. And the only way to do that is to experience a life on the Physical Plane. It's not enough to simply observe our world and hope to know what it's like to be here. To really find out what being human is all about, a soul has to leave the Universal Consciousness and become part of a physical body.

Once it does this, the game begins. The soul will then be here for a complete chain of lives, during which it will be exposed to everything the Physical Plane can throw at it".
("The Instruction" by Ainslie MacLeod)

The key to understanding this important concept is to stop, take a deep breath, and then accept that where you are now in your life is exactly where you are meant to be. You are perfect just as you are. No need to strive to be more than you already are. You are who you are meant to be and you are exactly where you need to be. All is exactly as it should be and there is no need to feel inferior, challenged or insecure. You are loved by the universe just for being who you are - and you are on the *right* path that is taking you to the *right* place. You are learning what you need to learn in order to progress on your journey and the lessons and challenges you have to face up to, however hard they might seem right now, can best be envisaged as stepping stones across a swamp. In other words you need courage to step from stone to stone in order to arrive safely at the other side of the swamp, but taking each brave step is always a better option than stepping off the path.

To understand what some of the these 'stepping stones' might challenge us with on our life's journey, let's now examine one of the hardest obstacles we ever have to face and deal with - our relationships!

Relationships in the Spiritual Context

At this point I need to say a little more about the subject of relationships because not only is this a huge subject in terms of our life here on the Earth Plane, but it is equally important in the bigger scheme of things, in the spiritual world. Not only that, but even more importantly, relationships are one of the few elements of our existence that bridge both worlds. We tend to think of our relationships as having relevance only in this lifetime because when we die our relationships come to a natural end. But in the spiritual context this is not so. Some relationships can continue for hundreds or even thousands of lives and I am not just referring to our relationship with our 'significant other' but in much wider terms.

Some of these relationship issues will be explored in more detail as we examine each of the seven stages of the soul in this book, but it is best to start with a few generalisations in order to properly set the scene for what is to follow.

We all know that relationships are one of the most fundamental and central elements of our life and include our relationships with our loved ones, our immediate family, our wider family, friends, colleagues and even the strangers we bump into on life's journey that leave an impression. But this is only half the story. In the spiritual realms we also have a relationship with our 'Chief Guide' (otherwise known as our Guardian Angel) plus many other guides charged to look after our wellbeing. But that's not all. We also have relationships with the members of our Soul Group, other associated Soul Groups, other Spiritual Teachers and of course, our ultimate relationship with Source - our original Mother/Father/Creator - our point of origin.

This means that when we try to make sense of relationship issues in our day-to-day existence on the Earth Plane we can only really comprehend the whole picture if we are prepared to consider those relationship issues from both the human (Earth Plane) viewpoint AND the spiritual (Soul) viewpoint. Both have equal validity and both need to be taken into account.

If we choose to exclude one or the other viewpoints then we are unlikely to find resolution because some answers will be Earth Plane related and other answers will be Spiritual World related. And this is a critically important point that needs to be fully understood. Let me try to give some examples to make this important point as clear as possible without going too deep into this vast topic.

Let's say there has been a breakdown of communication between two people and let's say they are a 'couple' (married or unmarried) on the Earth Plane. When a relationship of this nature breaks down both parties want to find answers. They want to understand why the relationship has come to a point where they can no longer live together and they are finding it increasingly difficult to communicate or find common ground. There can be many reasons for this happening, whether the couple have been together for two months or twenty years. Let's look at a few possible reasons for a relationship ending from both the Earth Plane and the Spirit World perspectives to make this point clearer.

Possible 'Earth Plane' reasons for a communication breakdown

- One partner no longer loves the other partner
- One partner has found a potential new partner
- They have been arguing over lots of things and can no longer find common ground
- Their life choices and life goals are no longer in sync with each other
- Wider family issues including children issues or relatives issues
- Arguments over money
- Religious or belief system differences

Possible 'Spirit World' reasons for a communication breakdown

- As part of their Soul Contract both parties agreed to stay together for a certain time on the Earth Plane and then part after a particular lesson has been fully learned
- To complete a 'karmic promise' (e.g. a karmic issue has now been fully resolved)
- Because an agreed Earth Plane challenge or obstacle has now been successfully overcome so their partnership now needs to end so that both souls can move on
- Because one partner has accelerated faster on their soul path than the other partner and they have now become spiritually incompatible

• Because both partners in the relationship needed to learn a specific lesson by being together and the lesson has now successfully been learned

These are just a few typical examples and are not exhaustive, but they do serve to demonstrate just how complex relationships can be when viewed *in totality* and not just from a one-sided limited perspective.

So, to continue with the example of the couple who are involved in a relationship break-up let's say, for the sake of argument, that one partner (whom we will call 'Dan') is a Level One soul who does not accept the reality of the Spiritual World and believes it is all airy-fairy nonsense. And the other partner (whom we will call 'Liz') has now progressed to a Level Five soul who knows without question that she is here on the Earth Plane to fulfil her life purpose and her Soul Contract.

How do they resolve their communication breakdown in order to resolve the situation? One partner, Dan, is arguing his case from the Earth Plane perspective and the other partner, Liz, is arguing her case from the Spirit World perspective. In their early days they were in love and enjoying just being together and everything seemed fine. But now Liz is accelerating much faster on her personal soul journey, but Dan, who is also progressing on his soul journey, is progressing at a much slower pace. They are both where they are meant to be and they are both learning the life lessons they are supposed to be learning - so in essence they are both in the right place at the right time. But on the Earth Plane things between them are not going well.

So, what about the perspective from the Spirit World?

Both Dan's spirit guides and Liz's spirit guides have a very clear purpose and they are both guiding their charges from a place of love and caring. Both Dan and Liz are beautiful unique souls on the Earth Plane for a specific purpose - to learn, to grow and to flourish - and a spirit guide's purpose is to ensure the soul they care for is nurtured and given space to mature.

Liz's spirit guide is delighted with Liz's progress on her soul journey and is now nudging Liz to move towards the next Stage of her soul evolution - Stage Six. And Dan's spirit guide is also gently nudging Dan to move towards his next challenge - to move from a Stage One soul to a Stage Two soul. But the spirit guides are both looking at Dan and Liz from the spiritual perspective of growth over thousands of lifetimes. Both of them have important lessons to learn on the Earth Plane and when one lesson has been fully learned then the next challenge is looming on the horizon. If both partners have now learned all the lessons they are supposed to have learned during their time together, it may well be that an ongoing relationship would only serve to hold both of them back from any further progression.

In other words, by forcing the relationship to endure on the Earth Plane rather than letting it come to a natural end when it is spiritually right for it to end, both partners will be stuck on their spiritual path and unable to move forward until the relationship is finally over.

Ending a relationship need not, and should not, be seen as or viewed as failure as a Level One soul would typically view it, but in a spiritual context should be seen as a natural end to an important life stage. The relationship has served its purpose and both souls are now free to continue their journeys as they agreed to do in their Soul Contract. There is no reason why the relationship should not continue - but it needs to be on a new footing as a lifelong friendship without animosity or blame - rather than continuing as an artificial or forced intimate connection.

In this example, Liz, as a Level Five soul will intuitively recognise this truth but will find it impossible to convince Dan. This is because, as a Level One soul, Dan will accuse Liz of talking rubbish and may never forgive her for ending the relationship. Also, as a higher level soul, Liz will know how to use the power of forgiveness for two important purposes. Firstly, to forgive Dan for not being able to fully understand the dynamics of the situation in the broader context and secondly in having the courage to forgive herself for causing hurt to Dan. In other words Liz has progressed to a level of soul maturity that recognises that forgiving Dan *and forgiving herself* is essential if she is to move on with her soul journey. In a sense it is like two people trying to communicate but speaking different languages. Neither person can make themselves heard or understood because their perspectives of what constitutes reality are so diametrically opposed.

This situation is not just relevant to a typical couple, however. All through life we will experience communication breakdowns with numerous people we interact with during our Earth Plane existence - whether friends, family or work colleagues. It is very easy for two Level One souls to communicate because they speak the same language. And is very easy for two Level Seven souls to communicate because they too will speak the same language. But trying to get more advanced souls to communicate effectively with less advanced souls is almost always likely to fail because there is no common foundation. And this is not a hierarchical judgement. It is simply a reflection of how the universe actually works.

Our relationships with others is a critical part of our life's experiences but it should not be viewed in isolation because we also have beautiful and enduring relationships in the spirit world too. There is, however, a fundamental difference. On the Earth Plane we are all having a human experience and that experience teaches us about how to deal with relationship issues relating to things like jealousy, deceit, selfishness, mistrust, anger, blame etc. But our relationships in the spiritual realm are very different.

We still experience all the positive emotions like love, compassion, intimacy and caring etc. but the more negative emotions are not present in the spiritual realm. This is because everything is open and transparent and nothing can be hidden - so it is impossible for a soul to lie or deceive or manipulate others. All souls that reside in the spiritual realms can instantly and effortlessly read each other's minds through what we call 'telepathy' so the destructive elements that affect relationships on the Earth Plane are not possible. Now that this element of relationships has been explained we can move on to explore some other important concepts relating to our soul journey.

The Ladder to the Stars

When we are first created out of Source and given the breath of life to grow and flourish we are totally pure souls, completely untarnished and innocent. And at the end of our soul's journey, maybe thousands of lives later, we are absorbed back into Source equally as pure. Source is always completely pure and tarnished souls cannot be accepted back to their Home until every last impurity has been removed. And, in a way, that is exactly why we need to go through so many incarnations and to grow and mature through all seven levels of experience. It is so that by the time we have reached seventh level - and experienced many lives as a seventh level soul - that our self-purification happens naturally.

This being said, though, the spiritual guides are always keen to clarify any misconceptions about what is meant by these terms 'pure' and 'tarnished' in order to avoid any misunderstandings. They want it to be clearly stated that ALL souls are welcomed 'home' after transition with love and joy and without judgement or prejudice. They are also very clear that any idea or belief about any form of 'Hell' is an old-fashioned medieval myth without any foundation. Any type of judgement relating to our deeds on the Earth Plane are always about our own self-judgement. In effect, in the period after transition, we become our own judge and jury when reflecting on our our most recent and other former lives. In simple terms, we learn and grow by reviewing and evaluating all our own mistakes. We don't need anyone else to criticise or judge us. Our own conscience is enough.

But the journey of our soul is not always a linear one. For many cultures across the world the soul's journey is depicted in different ways - but the images of ladders or stairways between earth and sky seems to be a common symbol to help people visualise this concept. The image of 'Jacob's ladder' in the Bible is a good example - as are many ancient Tibetan paintings of golden stairways leading forever upwards. Almost all pictures embrace the idea of ascension with the journey beginning on the first rung of a ladder or the first step of a staircase that leads to the magical kingdom above - whether we choose to call it 'Nirvana', 'Heaven', 'Source' or our 'Spiritual Home'.

The ladder is actually a good analogy for imagining having lived hundreds or thousands of previous lives with each rung of the ladder representing our next life as we climb forever upwards. In karmic terms some people believe we go up one rung each time we have lived a good life or down one rung if we have lived a bad life or somehow failed in our mission during this current life. But this is oversimplifying the reality of how soul progression really works. Neither our present life or our previous lives can be compared to the game of 'Snakes and Ladders' because our soul evolution is much more complex than this as we shall see during the rest of this book.

As Robert E. Cox explains in his book on the soul's journey:

"The layers of the living universe represent layers of consciousness, which can be understood as various universal fields of consciousness. The ancients compared the process of traversing these layers to the process of ascending (and descending) a divine ladder or stairway to the sky. Moreover, they understood this divine ladder or stairway as the path of immortality".
("Creating the Soul Body" by Robert E. Cox)

Many people who are privileged to be able to communicate or 'speak' to the spirit world regularly, (psychics, mediums, clairvoyants, channellers etc) have asked spirit about the accuracy of the concept of the 'Ladder to the Stars' and have received an interesting answer from the spirit world.

The usual answer from the spirit world is that using the ladder or stairway metaphor to teach spiritual truths is a good analogy when talking or teaching about our soul's journey and previous lives etc. but that the actual reality is slightly different because the true ladder is not rigid but flexible and is actually a spiral ladder that twists and turns in a similar way as the structure of DNA – the double helix. So, if we want a more precise mental image of our soul's journey then we should envisage a spiral ladder rather than a fixed, rigid and linear one.

The best way to visualise this is as an oval running track where the 'start line' is also the 'finish line'. After you have run one circuit (one life) and reached the finish line the track curves upwards for the second circuit (second life) and so on. The running track continues to spiral upwards all the way to Source. The reasons for this are apparently too complex for us to understand while we are living on the Earth Plane but are explained to us in more detail after transition to the spiritual realms (i.e. when we are between lives).

It seems that our spirit guides, whilst always there to help and support us, can only share certain things related to the knowledge of life in the spiritual realms while we are still in physical form on the Earth Plane. Other truths we have to wait for and can only be revealed when we are spiritually mature enough to be ready to accept them.

Many Precious Lives

The subject of reincarnation is vast and although it is undoubtedly a central theme in this book it is too complex in scope to be fully addressed in its entirety. Every year there are more and more books published on this topic with a steadily building body of evidence, both spiritual and increasingly scientific, that support the concept of the immortality of the soul. (See the Appendix for 'Recommended Reading'). The findings that are being made by researchers today are merely the rediscovery of an ancient truth that is in accord with spiritual teachings and observations that stretch back into far antiquity when such concepts were known intuitively and instinctively.

This book is focused on the Journey of the Soul and in Part Two it serves to analyse, in some depth, the seven steps that every single one of us must take in our constant spiritual evolution. It is, I believe, the reflection of a beautiful and elegant story that reveals a timeless truth that embodies both aspects of our unique journey on the path to ultimate enlightenment. I am speaking here about the two aspects of the journey that we all go through and that take place on both the Spiritual Plane and the Earth Plane.

Part Two of this book focuses predominantly on the Earth Plane phase of our journey whereas this section, in contrast, focuses more on the Spiritual Plane aspect in order to explain the characteristics of both experiences. To fully understand the journey of the soul through the Spiritual Realm of existence though, requires a totally different approach to understanding the soul's journey on the Earth Plane. The two modes of existence are very different and whereas we can examine our journey on the Earth Plane through the medium of direct experience - that we can all relate to as Earth dwellers - we must take a very different approach when we examine the nature of the spiritual realms.

In order to understand what happens to our immortal soul after death, or 'transition', we have to rely on a variety of wisdom sources that bridge the gap between our earthly existence and our existence on the higher vibrational planes. Traditionally, this has been achieved by using the abilities of a group of unique individuals who have been blessed with the ability to communicate with the spiritual realms. We call such individuals Shamans or Psychics, Mediums or Visionaries, Religious 'Wisdom Keepers', Soothsayers, Sages and Gurus, Spiritual Healers and Masters, Wizards and Witches, Wise Ones or Elders etc. There are many words for those extraordinary individuals who are born with the ability to pierce the veil and communicate with the other side.

But for the more sceptical inquirer who doubts the abilities of such extraordinary individuals there is also a new breed of wisdom seekers who approach the question of the afterlife with a very different approach. Today, we have an increasing number of highly qualified and highly respected hypnotherapists who are trained to induce a light trance to help people overcome fears and phobias created somewhere in their past - usually in early childhood. Over recent years however, as regression therapy has become more widespread, many of these experienced hypnotherapists have had clients slipping into a light trance and reporting not just incidents from their childhood but also very detailed incidents from their past lives.

Sceptics will, of course, put this down to imagination or delusion - but over the years thousands upon thousands of case studies have led to past life claims being intensely scrutinised and checked - only to find that these past lives can be forensically verified. Names, dates, incidents and obscure facts are proven to be true over and over again which are derived from both adults and children. This abundance of evidence has now led to many hypnotherapists becoming specialists in past life healing and they are now more commonly called 'Past Life Regressionists'. In simple terms they focus on helping clients to overcome traumas buried in their subconscious, not just from childhood incidents, but also from many past life incidents that need to be revisited through the medium of trance in order to understand them, process them and then heal and recover.

The Appendix lists many of these sources but I want to highlight in particular the extraordinary body of work conducted by regressionists like Michael Newton, Brian Weiss, Suzanne Giesemann and 'Near Death Experience' (NDE's) specialists like Ray Moody and Eben Alexander who have opened up new doors of enquiry and also opened our eyes into the verifiable truth of past lives.

Based on the findings of these Past Life Regressionists we now have a very clear window into what actually happens after death or transition. And when thousands of individuals from different cultural backgrounds and with different belief systems, viewpoints, religions and traditions all tell the same story when under hypnosis, then we have to sit up, listen and learn.

So this next section is a very brief and very 'high level' introduction to what happens to our soul upon leaving the body at the time of transition until the next reincarnation (literally 'born again'). It is based upon the experiences and findings of these talented regressionists who have diligently recorded what their clients are reporting about life 'between lives' when our soul has completed one incarnation and is now temporarily resident in the spiritual realm awaiting the next rebirth.

So let's now take a brief foray into this shadow world that we all have to traverse as part of our own journey, for it describes a place we know so well that when under hypnosis we simply refer to it as 'Home'.

Most of us are familiar with what might be termed the first stage of transition or what we commonly term physical death of the body. In the simplest of terms this is the end of life as we know it, and in medical terminology is the point at which our physical life ends and the process of death begins. The subject of death in clinical, medically acceptable terms, would require a whole book in its own right and the purpose of this book is not to cover this vast topic. Suffice to say, that in rational, scientific terms death is the cessation of our consciousness and our normal bodily functions. Our breathing stops, our physical body 'dies' and 'life is over'.

But as far as the spiritual world is concerned the word 'death' has no meaning because it is merely a transition point where the physical body - which has simply been borrowed as a vessel for this particular incarnation - is discarded so that the immortal soul can once more be released in order to return to its temporary home on the spiritual plane for the next stage of its journey. The natural miracle of the caterpillar and the butterfly is the perfect analogy for understanding this concept. The caterpillar outwardly dies and is entombed in a hard chrysalis with no concept that it will shortly be reborn as a beautiful butterfly that soars through the air to new heavenly gardens.

The Soul's Journey
from the Earth Plane
to the Spiritual Plane

Transition and Departure

At the moment of death, or shortly after, the immortal soul leaves the physical body as it has done many times before. The temporarily borrowed physical body is no longer required and the soul is now free once more. At first, this transition can be very confusing and sometimes distressing for the released soul. Shortly after transition the soul starts to have an awareness of being a 'form' rather than a body which causes a degree of shock and anxiety but this soon turns to a feeling of calm and fascination. There is a sensation of floating and an awareness of non-solidity, lightness of being and freedom from all pain or discomfort. The soul can clearly see any people who are still in the room with the physical body, but also becomes aware that communication with those people is not possible because they are unaware of the soul's presence (although in many cases, some family members who have a particular sensitivity do indeed feel the presence of the soul around them).

After an indeterminate time the soul starts to realise that it is still 'alive', albeit in a different form, and the previous fear of death has now dissipated and been replaced with a sense of some kind of wonder, familiarity and continuity. After a while the soul starts to feel a sort of magnetic pull and realises there is some kind of energy steering it in a specific direction away from the physical room and physical body. All fear has now gone and the soul is now feeling more relaxed and curious. There is a sense of freedom coupled with a sense that there are other souls floating around somewhere nearby.

Through the Threshold

The second stage of transition starts with the full acceptance that physical death has occurred and the full awareness of the 'soul body' which has survived death and is now capable of thought, self-awareness and freedom of movement. The sensation of being pulled away from the physical body has now become stronger and the soul now discovers it can move freely through solid objects like walls and houses.

The soul realises it is being gently pulled towards the entrance of a large translucent tunnel or funnel which is very wide and is almost always described as having shimmering walls of pure light. There is an intuitive sense that this is where the soul needs to go and without any sense of fear the soul effortlessly drifts into the mouth of the tunnel and feels a sense of being pulled upwards. Within the tunnel is a bright white mist, a deep silence and an awareness of other 'thoughts' being transmitted from other previously departed souls to the newly released soul. These 'thought forms' express emotions like love, compassion, empathy, reunion, peace and 'welcome home'. The soul ascends the glowing tunnel and becomes aware of a brilliant and intense light at the far end of the tunnel. Regression clients then report a strange nostalgic feeling of returning to their natural home accompanied by a deepening awareness of who they truly are and why they are here.

Going 'Home'

As the soul becomes more comfortable with its new found freedom from the restrictions of the physical body it also becomes more aware that it is not alone. There is a gradual recognition that there are many other souls in close proximity. These other souls are manifested as glowing points of light that also contain consciousness and they are also travelling upwards through the tunnel of light. The soul intuitively knows that these other lights are fellow travellers who have also recently departed their physical bodies.

It is usually at this point that the soul's Guardian Angel first appears and there is a joyful reunion. It is the Guardian Angel's prime responsibility to welcome the beloved soul home and the soul instantly recognises his or her Guardian Angel as the one who has been nurturing them through countless lifetimes. This is a time of incredible emotion as the reunion occurs. It is often reported that the Guardian Angel is sometimes accompanied at this point by other souls from the spiritual realms who are usually previously departed loved ones, family members or relatives. The Guardian Angel and other souls known to the newly departed soul then continue the journey through the tunnel together until they arrive at a certain point where the soul is met and welcomed by other very important souls who have been an integral part of the soul's journey through thousands of incarnations. These are principally the soul's eternal 'soul mates' and possibly 'twin flames' that have already transitioned, plus other deceased family members and relatives.

These other souls are essentially a 'welcoming party' but they stay only briefly to provide initial comfort. When this beautiful reunion happens the soul's Guardian Angel usually waits and watches from a distance as if respectfully allowing the soul time to reintegrate with his or her loved ones. When the reunion has been completed the Guardian Angel then fulfils their next responsibility - which is to take the newly departed soul to meet their 'Soul Group' for another emotional reunion. The Soul Group is composed of a team of approximately fifteen to thirty souls who are at the same level of soul maturity as the newly departed soul. The Guardian Angel has particularly orchestrated this important meeting and reunion. In essence the soul has now been reunited with his or her very closest friends - those travelling on their soul journeys in parallel and at broadly the same pace. These individuals have been - and still are - the soul's timeless companions on the great journey.

Re-orientation

This initial meeting with the Soul Group is only a quick reunion as many more meetings are to follow shortly, where there is real work to be done. The most important priority now (following the re-orientation meetings with deceased loved ones, soul mates and the soul group) is for the Guardian Angel to escort the newly departed soul, alone, to a place known as 'The Place of Healing'. At this location the soul is bathed in pure white light which serves to cleanse, re-energise and re-balance the soul to its original state of purity.

This action is the same for all returning souls and is done to essentially decontaminate the soul from unwanted 'pollutants' and to remove any remaining defective 'human traces' brought from the Earth Plane. This seems to be a pre-requisite energy-bathing and balancing ritual that ensures the spiritual plane remains free from any potential contaminants. After the completion of this ritual the Guardian Angel then escorts the purified soul to meet other spiritual guides ('Teachers' and 'Mentors' etc) for an initial de-briefing and rehabilitation session. This important meeting involves what might be termed a 'deep counselling' session which has been described as 'open, firm and probing' in which nothing can be hidden from the guides and where all life-decisions taken during the last incarnation on the Earth Plane are thoroughly and constructively examined, dissected and discussed. This meeting and discussion, which is always conducted with love and without any type of judgement or criticism, includes a deep discussion of the soul's purpose on the Earth Plane and a review of the all-important Soul Contract. This is where the soul has to face up to some hard questions including, 'Were all the designated life lessons really learned during the last incarnation?', 'Were all the challenges truly faced and overcome?' and most importantly of all, 'Has this soul learned enough to progress to the next stage of its soul journey or do they need to return and go through it all again?'

Reunion

After the initial full debrief and discussion with the Spirit Teachers has been completed, the Guardian Angel then escorts the soul to a different place in order to provide a time of rest, recuperation and deep relaxation for the soul to think, reflect and analyse all that it has experienced thus far. This relaxation time is very important for the soul to fully experience a period of peace and safety in order to fully assimilate all that it has learned. This is a time of re-acquaintance with the spiritual realms and to acknowledge its identity as an immortal spirit traversing many lifetimes. It is a time to reflect on what has been learned or maybe not-yet-learned in terms of the Soul Contract and also to reflect on the previous life on the Earth Plane. Deep rest and self-introspection is vital at this stage of the soul's journey.

When the soul's Guardian Angel feels the time is right, the soul will then be escorted to another place within the spiritual realms. This place has been described by thousands of souls as a sort of 'staging area' which is like the hub of an enormous slowly spinning wheel with windows around the outer wheel rim. The view outside of the 'windows' is of the universe i.e. deep space with radiant stars and galaxies. But inside the wheel the multitude of rooms around the wheel rim are all full of beautiful light. There are huge amphitheatre type rooms and many smaller classroom type rooms where thousands of souls (light beings) work together in their own soul groups.

At the centre hub of the wheel is a huge domed area which many souls describe as reminding them of a vast airport or rail terminal. Each spoke of the wheel also has many classrooms full of souls, and there are also many corridors where thousands of souls float - rather than walk - along as though being carried by a gently flowing sea current from place to place.

All souls are visible as glowing lights but they are all of different vibrant and translucent colours where each colour reflects the soul's level of maturity. For example, most souls are pure white, Teachers and mentors are yellow and the 'Council of Elders' are mostly purple. Each soul works in a kind of classroom with his or her own soul group. For hundreds or possibly thousands of years each soul group has been reunited following their individual Earth Plane life experiences and there is a strong sense of a universal bond or 'oneness' within the group members and the sense of regularly being together for eternity. Each soul group is composed of between 10-20 souls and there may be seven or eight soul groups within one 'Soul Cluster'. The other groups that together form a Soul Group Cluster are all closely linked to the specific soul group to which a single soul is assigned - but there are many familiar faces in the other groups that form a specific cluster. To understand this better, the soul group can be likened to a bunch of very close friends while there are other soul groups that have lots of other more distant friends and acquaintances. Together these connected soul groups form one 'Cluster Group'.

There are hundreds of other clusters all containing soul groups, but these are composed of strangers who are unfamiliar. Every soul that is in your own soul group (i.e. your closest soul friends) are addressed not by their Earth Plane name, which is very incarnation specific, but by their unique 'soul name' which is an eternal name that never changes throughout every incarnation (this eternal soul name has been described as actually more of a 'sound' than a word). This is an important point. During each incarnation our parents give us a name which we retain for one single life. But when we return to our 'home' between lives, everyone there knows us by our 'eternal name' which is our unique soul name that is retained forever. Some people on the Earth Plane are intuitively able to recall their soul name and recognise it as being the essence of who they are, but for most of us it remains forgotten until we transition and are welcomed back.

Reviews and Learnings

The 'schoolrooms' mentioned above seat around 15 souls and each group of souls has a Guide or Teacher overseeing them and conducting each learning session. In addition to the work undertaken in the classroom setting - which is composed of a close-knit intimate group of souls at the same maturity level - there is also a much larger room referred to as 'The Library'. This huge library has been described as being very similar to an ancient Greek temple with many beautifully carved circular pillars and many tables which can be used for study. The shelves are filled with books but they are not made from paper. They are described as all being individual 'movies' similar to videos or dvds but being made of 'light' and multi-dimensional. Each 'book' can be taken from the shelf and watched by the book's 'owner' because it contains a visual record of not just the soul's last incarnation, but also the visual film records of all the soul's past lives. All these past lives can be watched and analysed based on learning about the consequences of all the choices made during each and every incarnation. These books are basically learning tools that hold the complete records of all the incarnations of each and every soul. They are therefore a complete and accurate record of how every life has been led and how the soul is progressing on its unique learning journey. It is important to note that these records (sometimes referred to as the 'Akashic Records') are never used in a critical or judgemental way. The objective is for the Teachers to work with all souls, individually and as a group to simply learn and reflect on the consequences of choices made on the Earth Plane during each incarnation.

Learning is facilitated by both the soul's Guardian Angel and other Teachers because the Guardian Angel has always been present to guide their soul through every incarnation. After analysis of the movie-books, a discussion then takes place within the soul group which may well include previous partners, husbands, wives, lovers, children, parents, relations, close friends etc. There is lots of open discussion in a good humoured positive way because everything is open and visible to all. There can be no falsehoods or lies because there are only pure souls taking part. All the egos have been left behind in the physical body. Almost every soul that has described this process makes the point that living on planet Earth is always considered the biggest challenge of all and although many lessons are learned during incarnations on other planets the tasks are generally much easier than on Earth. In fact, Earth is considered the 'ultimate challenge' because of the nature of the ego and the issues created when inhabiting a human body with the associated human emotions. It is also worth mentioning that all souls using the library and going through these life reviews with their Teachers and Guardians, consider this time spent in the Spiritual Realms as the true reality and the Earth Plane reality as merely an illusion.

Planning and Commitment

After the required time has been spent on the life-review teachings in the library and there has been sufficient involvement in both the soul group sessions and one-to-one sessions with Teachers or Guardians the time comes when the soul has learned enough. Sometimes though, higher level guides normally referred to as the 'Council of Elders' are involved. At the end of this period of relaxation and review there is a basic question that must always be asked which determines the next stage of the individual soul's evolution. The question is simple: "Is this soul now ready to progress to a higher level or do they need to go back and try again?". Such is the nature of the law of karma.

Unless the soul has made a significant breakthrough - which does happen to us all at some point or other on our journey - the chances are that we need to return to the Earth Plane for yet another incarnation in a new body. Now the time has come to start the preparations for the next step on the soul's journey involving a lot of decisions made by both the soul and his or her Guardian Angel. A new life selection is a critically important decision involving discussions about place, time, body, sex, parents, and, most importantly, the challenges and the obstacles which will need to be overcome. This involves both dress-rehearsals and watching more book-movies in advance that reveal a series of different options and scenarios. But these are always 'observation only' potential scenarios which cannot ever be manipulated.

There are lots of 'pre-body' preparations with the soul group all involved in the discussions and decision making. Eventually a new life is selected and all the players are introduced who will play important parts in the next life (like the cast of a film meeting for rehearsals). Challenges and obstacles are agreed, learning goals are defined, options are discussed and key decisions agreed upon. In effect, this is the point where each of us plans and agrees what our next life will be and how it will be played out - regardless of how we might use our free will to modify or change that plan when back in our physical body on the Earth Plane. At this stage souls about to embark on this new incarnation will be asking questions like, "Will I meet with my soul mate again?" or "Will this new life be easier or harder than last time around?'. Relationships are a key and essential part of the soul lessons which are in effect a 'karmic test'. When everything has been agreed and accepted there is then a final de-brief and review. The Teachers and Guides will usually then remind the soul of the importance of human eyes as the key organs for soul group recognition indicators on the Earth Plane. When everything is ready there will be a last visit to the Council of Elders for the soul to agree and approve the final objectives of the forthcoming Soul Contract and then, inevitably, some emotional goodbye's with the soul's Guardian Angel, Soul Group, Twin Flames and Soul Mates. Finally, the prepared soul will be escorted to the point of embarkation to be left alone, nervous and excited and ready for the next incarnation.

Rebirth

In mid to late pregnancy the 'old' soul enters the body of the new baby and gradually gets to know his new host. The soul at this point is well aware of everything that has passed and this knowledge remains until the moment of physical birth when a spiritually induced amnesia is initiated. This is to protect both the soul and the brain of the new baby from being mentally overloaded. Over the next few months the soul gets to know his new host and the baby is also aware of the soul's presence - although this awareness fades over time as the baby develops its own personality.

Some people, especially new mothers, find this last statement very difficult to comprehend. The very idea of their beautiful new baby being 'inhabited' by an 'old soul' seems a rather macabre statement. But once fully understood and when spiritual logic is applied, rather than Earth Plane logic, the concept has a very different meaning. Every new baby *does* develop its own unique personality and that is absolutely essential for soul growth. The parents were very carefully chosen by the spiritual Elders to have the honour of receiving a beautiful and pure soul to unite with the baby's unique personality. That bond is very special and is something to be appreciated for the wonderful potential that has been created.

Before leaving this section of the book there are a couple of important points that need to be mentioned.

Firstly, many people ask the question, "How long do we stay in the spiritual realm between lives?". The answer to this question is that the concept of time in the spiritual realm is totally different from Earth bound time. It is so different that the question is actually irrelevant because spiritual time cannot be measured in a linear way. So the answer to the question is actually, 'As long as it takes to recover from the previous life and prepare for the next life', which is specific to each individual soul. This may feel like days, months or years but is actually immeasurable.

The second point is to do with religion. In some religions there is a cultural expectation of what the afterlife will bring. In the Christian connotation, for example, devout Christians' may well expect to meet Angels, Jesus, Saints and perhaps even God in somewhere called 'heaven'. Other religions including the Buddhist, Hindu and Moslem traditions will also have culturally derived 'expectations'.

When regressed clients are asked about this topic the answer is always consistent and unambiguous. There is 'no religion' in the afterlife. Every soul is respected for whatever belief or religion they have chosen to follow on the Earth Plane but in the spiritual realms all souls are 'equal' and the concept of following a particular religion does not exist. However, and this is an important point, many individuals who have experienced 'Near Death Experiences' (NDE's) *do* report having seen religious entities that have comforted them before being recalled into their bodies. It is very clear that the spiritual realms always tries to comfort souls experiencing NDE's by meeting their expectations of the afterlife in a way that is in accord with their religious beliefs. But this is temporary comfort only. Once full transition has taken place these religious figures are very rarely or never experienced.

This section would not be complete without reference to another phenomenon of past-life regressions. Over many years of regressing thousands of individuals to their past life experiences a large number of the regressed will describe, in great detail, lives spent on other planets in other forms of being. This is so common that it is no longer considered a 'rare' or anomalous occurrence but rather something that occurs naturally to many people.

Past-life regressionists have coined the term 'Interplanetary Souls' or 'IP's' for such people who are able to describe their life on another planet as effortlessly and calmly as a 'normal' life on planet earth. And, from the information gleaned from such sessions, it seems that in the spiritual realms, experiencing lives in different life-forms on different planets can be an extremely rewarding experience for all souls who experience it. It is simply another learning opportunity or schoolroom for a developing and maturing soul.

This is a huge topic in itself and outside the scope of this book. However there is one aspect of the IP past-life that is definitely worth mentioning. Experiencing life on a different planet from Earth is considered by the spirit world to be an invaluable lesson for all souls because they are exposed to a radically and totally different type of life in a different body and within a different culture with different values and belief systems. So when an IP soul transitions from an off-Earth life and is then reborn on Earth the 'culture-shock' can be severe and have a number of consequences, both positive and negative. These revelations often emerge during the past-life regression sessions where the individual is in a light trance and able to speak freely and openly about things they might otherwise never want to reveal.

On the positive side an IP soul will have a much wider breadth of experience to call upon as they continue to mature spiritually. In other words, not only do they have the accumulated wisdom gathered over many Earth-based lives but this is supplemented by the wisdom accumulated during their off-Earth lives. This broader experience often gives them a more open and tolerant view of life in its widest context and literally in its universal context. There is likely to be more compassion for all people regardless of colour or creed and less prejudice for example.

On the 'negative side', however, many IP souls who have enjoyed life on a planet where there is no war, no disease, no violence, no poverty and less ego-driven behaviours, find it extremely difficult to adjust to an Earth-based existence. They may find it impossible to 'fit in' to life on Earth and tend to become shy or withdrawn, over-sensitive, depressed or confused. They are effectively 'strangers in a strange land' and it is clear that some IP souls are able to cope much better than others. In spiritual terms, this situation is the whole point of the experience. In the wider scheme of things, the spirit world informs us that this is all part of the soul's learning journey. In order to become a truly wise soul, life can never be a bed of roses without us being prepared to feel the thorns. To ascend through the levels and to become a seventh level soul it may be necessary for us to experience the whole breadth of the spectrum - from dwelling on a peace loving planet where no aggression exists - to experiencing life on the front-line in an earthly war zone.

For anyone specifically interested in learning more about IP souls I recommend reading the excellent book, "Souls on Earth" by Doctor Linda Backman, which is included in the 'Recommended Reading' section at the end of the book.

The Taming of the Ego

U nderstanding the nature of the ego is probably the most important message in this entire book. And the reason for this statement is very simple. The 'journey of the soul' is not just a journey in terms of moving from A to B through incarnations on the Earth Plane and the Spiritual Plane. It is also a journey that has a specific purpose and is a learning experience that we must all undertake in order to become enlightened. But what does that actually mean? What is enlightenment? And what is the *purpose* of enlightenment?

If it could be summed up in the most simple way possible, the answer to the question 'What is enlightenment?' is this: 'To conquer the ego'. But what does this also mean in real terms?

Conquering the ego is about firstly recognising and accepting the power our individual ego has over us - and how it dominates our lives, our thoughts and our actions. And secondly, to successfully conquer the ego is to recognise that until we can master and gain control over our ego we remain a slave to it and cannot therefore achieve spiritual independence. In other words, the purpose of our life, and the purpose of our soul journey, is to recognise the ego for what it is and to find the inner strength to take mastery over it. If we truly wish to accelerate our spiritual development and speed up our soul journey then taming the ego is by far the quickest way to achieve this goal.

At this point there is a very important distinction that needs to be understood before we can move on to explore the nature of the ego in more depth. The important distinction relates to the two aspects of the soul journey and how they affect the ego.

Essentially, when we are living an incarnation in our Earth body - i.e. in physical form - and in 'normal life', our ego is the dominant force controlling our feelings and actions. When we transition and our soul returns to the spiritual realms for a well earned rest between lives our ego is always left behind in the decaying physical body. It is not taken with us. It is a universal law than nothing impure can be imported into the spiritual realms because it would be a contaminant. We arrive into a new body as a pure soul and we return to the spiritual realms as a pure soul. So ego is simply an Earth Plane phenomenon. Our soul does not need it in the spirit world - so it is always left behind.

Now that this distinction is clear we can move on to examine the affect of the ego on our many lives and discover why the control of the ego should not only be our main goal in this and every life - but it is also key to our onward spiritual progression.

So what is this thing called the 'ego' that is holding us back on our soul journey and why is it such a big issue?

In the simplest of terms the ego is something that we all mistakenly identify as our personal identity even though, in reality, it is not our identity at all. So, in essence the ego can be likened to an imposter who is pretending to be you. Our one and only true identity is our immortal soul which is the only identity we ever need and which we carry from incarnation to incarnation. In fact the *only* thing we carry from one incarnation to another is our immortal soul and its inherent unique identity. When our immortal soul is incarnated into a newly created physical body in the form of a new born baby its presence cannot be detected by any scientific analysis but it is always there as the hidden core of consciousness.

But the immortal soul is not the only 'presence' within the new baby. The baby brings with its physical body a fully-functioning brain and awareness of 'self' that we call consciousness. And as the baby develops into a child, and then an adult, that conscious awareness also develops and matures as we learn and grow.

The ego also grows as we grow, from childhood to adulthood, even though few of us are consciously aware of its influence. Its objective is to control us and direct us to do as it wishes. The ego always believes that it is one hundred percent 'right' and is not interested in other people's opinions or ideas. It instils in us the belief that we are a totally separate and disconnected entity from others and that we are also the most important person in the universe. Spiritual traditions that are centuries old fully understand the nature of the ego and why it needs to be tamed if we are to develop spiritually. That is why the ego is known as 'Maya' in Hinduism meaning 'the veil of delusion' or 'Dukkha' in Buddhism meaning 'suffering'.

The ego is a problem not just in the sense of how we deal with it as an individual, but also in the much wider sense of society as a whole. Trying to tame one ego is hard enough, but when there is a 'collective ego' to be dealt with it is not just the individual who suffers - it is all living things. This is because the collective ego deems itself to be more important than anything else, just as the individual ego believes it is supremely important in a selfish way. The ego will do anything to protect itself and it does this through a very deliberate strategy which is to constantly strive to maintain control by filling our minds with endless thoughts. And just as the individual ego strives to control the body it resides within, so the global human species collective ego strives to control everything about the planet it lives on.

This egoic state of consciousness is sadly driving our planet to extinction, which is likely to become more prevalent and more dysfunctional as time goes on - leading ultimately to the breakdown of society and global chaos. Only a global awakening of consciousness can change this road to destruction, which means that every single one of us needs to recognise the influence our ego has on us and then understand why we need to deprive it of its power. Some advanced souls come back to the Earth Plane as volunteers just for this single purpose - to help ordinary people to understand the nature of the ego and why it needs to be tamed. Part of their mission is also to help raise the consciousness of other souls who are making good progress on their path to assist in this goal and the term 'Lightworkers' is sometimes given to these spiritually-oriented volunteers.

It is important to understand that when certain thoughts proliferate in the 'collective psyche' they can distort our perceptions of reality as well as our perceptions of what is true and untrue. This is why, unlike indigenous people who regard the Earth and nature as sacred, we continue to severely damage our planet and treat it as a resource we are free to exploit as we wish. It is because, collectively, we have been taught to believe that we are 'masters' of the Earth and can therefore treat everything that is not 'us' as free to plunder. The same is true when it comes to our beliefs about our own identity. We instinctively choose to identify with those other egos who think as we think. They are our 'friends'. So other egos that think differently to us must therefore, by definition, be 'enemies' or 'others'. So our egos are not just destroying our planet they are also responsible for creating an 'us and them' mentality which is the perfect recipe for ongoing global conflict.

As Eckhart Tolle so elegantly puts it:

"The ego needs an enemy for its continued survival. The ego strengthens itself by identifying the 'otherness' of others. Hence its refusal to compromise".
("A New Earth" by Eckhart Tolle)

We commit violence not just against each other but also against the environment and nature. We are literally biting the hand that feeds us. Driven by ego and greed we remain ignorant of our connectedness to the 'whole' and we are therefore the architects of our own destruction. As long as we cling to the illusion of separation as a species, the more we will destroy our planet and destroy ourselves.

The belief that we can solve global issues by science and technology or by making small token gestures to protect the environment like cutting carbon emissions or reducing plastic waste the more we continue to delude ourselves. These are laudable goals for sure, but unless the whole of mankind works together, as one, to jointly tackle these problems the impact will be minimal and ineffective. Only be applying 'unity consciousness' to global problems can we hope to turn things around. Only when we recognise that animals, insects, trees, plants, air, water and minerals are 'part' of us and not separate from us can we start to heal our global wounds and start to repair the damage. Part of our spiritual learning needs to be about recognising that, as a species, we suffer more deaths at the hands of each other than we ever do through natural disasters.

So, the enemy of enlightenment is ego. This is because ego identifies with itself by maintaining control of the 'voice in your head' and also maintaining control of your 'thought forms' - in other words your internal perception of what *is* and what *is not* reality. This self-centred focus of the ego is the main thing that disconnects us from both unity consciousness and the awareness that we are all intimately connected to everything else - including our connection to 'Source'. Until we can learn to silence, or at least ignore, the constant interference of the ego we will not be able to truly find inner contentment, peace, liberation and enlightenment. Ultimately, as each of us learns to control the ego as we follow our spiritual path, the ego will eventually self-implode, disintegrate and dissolve - as will all corrupt organisations, corporations and governments that can only survive whilst egoistic thinking is allowed to proliferate and dominate.

In the spirit world there are no egos. They are left behind when we transition. That means nothing can be hidden. There can be no lies. No manipulation of the truth. No falsehoods. We are all pure, unadulterated and totally transparent souls working together for the common good. And because every soul residing within the spiritual realm manifests this egoless state of being, then truth, unconditional love, compassion, tolerance, gratitude and selfless caring are able to flourish unchallenged.

Going back to the role of the ego on the 'Earth Plane' some might wonder why we have an ego at all if it is so destructive? Although we may never know the full answer to this question we can at least turn to ancient spiritual traditions in search of the answer. And the answer we find from ancient Hindu and Tibetan texts is that all souls need to experience obstacles and challenges in their life in order to evolve and grow. An egoic life is therefore a necessary pre-cursor in order for us to ultimately appreciate and understand the truth of an awakened consciousness. So, in essence, the message is very clear. Having an ego is a 'test' for all of us. We are given an ego in order to learn to master and overcome its dominance because then, and only then, can we transcend its influence and subdue its hold over us. The reward for doing so is ultimately spiritual enlightenment and fulfilment.

Once again Eckhart Tolle sums it up perfectly:

"You cannot fight the ego. Trying to fight it would be a waste of time. You have to acknowledge it, accept it for what it is and then observe it impartially. It is <u>not</u> you, but it <u>will</u> try to control you. The ego is only 'countered' by an awakened consciousness".
("A New Earth" by Eckhart Tolle)

So the obvious question at this point is, 'How *do* we learn to master the ego?'. The answer is that we need to first learn how to silence our constantly chattering so-called, 'monkey mind'. In other words we need to learn how to silence the voice in our head that tries to make all our decisions for us. This is the voice that judges what is right and what is wrong and criticises everything we do in our life - as well as criticising what others do in their lives if we consider it 'wrong' or not in accord with our own views! Most of us have got so used to our ego being in control of us that we don't even realise how we are being manipulated and this revelation can come as a terrible shock. The good news is that once we acknowledge and recognise the presence of our ego we are half way to silencing it, in order that the 'real' soul can then start to take back control by subduing the ego's dominance.

The best, but not the only way, of doing this is by stilling the mind's chatter by practising meditation or mindfulness. It is when we learn to still our mind and take charge of our thoughts that the ego can be overcome. It is beyond the scope of this book to delve deeply into the subject of meditation and ego-control but in high level terms the best way to start taking mastery of the ego is by consciously training yourself to become an 'observer' rather than a 'slave' to the ego. This is a four stage process which is very simple to explain, but may take years to achieve. However, it is definitely worth the effort.

The four stage process works like this: Firstly, you need to learn, accept and recognise that you have an ego that fills your head with thoughts every day of your life and thereby acts as a sort of barrier that stops you from accessing your deeper self (your soul). You need to openly acknowledge this as a true fact if you want to progress to the next stage of the exercise.

Secondly, shut your eyes and go somewhere quiet where you can fully relax. The next part of the exercise is the most difficult and needs perseverance to master. Start by mentally placing your conscious awareness of your true 'self' within your head at the back of your skull. It is important that you mentally place your awareness right at the back of the skull and not in the middle of the skull. Mentally identify yourself as 'The Observer' because you have now placed yourself in the position of 'Master'. You are, in other words, moving your conscious awareness away from the ego's control to a new manager - your true immortal soul. This step is key and may take time to get right so you need to persevere.

Thirdly, visualise the location of the ego as being right in the very centre of your skull immediately behind the eyes. What you have now effectively done is placed your 'true' self *behind* the ego as the ego looks out from your eyes. So now, in effect, you can watch the actions of your ego impartially (without becoming involved) and also from a detached point of view. The ego is no longer in charge because you, as 'The Observer', have taken control and you are now simply observing what your ego is thinking and doing from a more independent and non-judgemental viewpoint.

Fourthly, as you watch the constantly chattering ego create thought after thought, make the decision to refuse to be influenced by all these annoying thoughts. Treat them as you would wasps buzzing around your head. Mentally capture each thought that the ego creates, wrap a visualised 'balloon' around each thought and then watch as hundreds of balloons float out from the top of the skull and up into the sky to be gone forever. Do this exercise with minimum effort. Simply observe each thought the ego creates, mentally wrap it in a bubble and then *let it go.* You are now in control.

Over time this simple exercise can change your life because, if you can ignore the ego's manufactured thoughts and let them go without becoming involved with them, then your immortal soul - your true self - can start to gain dominance over the ego and the results will be life-changing.

Why is this exercise so powerful? It is because access to your soul is found in the gap between your thoughts. It really is as simple but profound as that. The ego does not want you to gain access to your soul because, if you do, then the ego loses its power over you. So the ego deliberately fills your mind with mind-chatter so that there is never a pause for your conscious mind to quickly slip between the chain of thoughts and gain access to your deeper self. But when we learn to silence the ego's stream of thoughts by capturing them in a metaphorical balloon or bubble and simply releasing them as soon as they are formed, without dwelling on them, we then get a chance to slip between them and get in touch with our soul. And that's when the magic starts.

At this point, however, the importance of humility needs to be mentioned because ego and humility cannot exist together. Our ego is focused on making itself supremely important. Our humility, by way of contrast, is focused on acknowledging our vulnerabilities and shortcomings by recognising that, although we may be 'perfect souls' in the universal context, we are also less than perfect humans on the Earth Plane. This means that we cannot become a better or wiser person just by wishing it to happen. Change has to come from within; so instead of trying to find or adopt 'goodness' from somewhere outside of us, it is better to find the goodness that is already residing within us by changing our mindset and attitude and by doing everything we can to raise our level of consciousness.

It is the same with wanting to become a more spiritual person. We cannot just wish it to happen or try to force it. The spirit world can never be rushed or manipulated. Our spiritual progression can only ever happen naturally. That being said, if we truly desire to speed up our progression on the spiritual path for the right reasons, then learning to control our ego is the essential prerequisite.

Do not be fooled into thinking you can buy spiritual development by going to expensive courses with fancy titles, by mastering complex yoga positions or surrounding yourself with incense sticks. This is pseudo-spirituality. True spiritual awareness does not demand that you do anything other than just '*be*' your true self i.e. your immortal soul-self and not your ego-self. The secret of success in taming the restless ego is actually very simple and is a twofold process - but it takes courage and determination to succeed. Firstly, you need to practice sincere forgiveness by learning to *truly* forgive yourself for separating your spiritual core-self from the universe by listening to the ego instead of your intuitions. Secondly, learn to sincerely thank the universe for all the lessons you have learned - and are still learning - with humility and acceptance. Both of these actions can be achieved through silence and meditation.

For many people who are new to these concepts it will undoubtedly take time to adjust to these new ways of thinking. For some, it may take many years to fully assimilate this new type of knowledge because our Earth Plane model of reality is so different. For centuries the word 'spirituality' has had a religious context and 'spiritual' was a word that conjured up images of Christian angels, churches, prayers, hymns, Buddha, various saints, gods or goddesses, mosques and temples etc. It is only within certain cultures and belief systems that spirituality was equated with the afterlife, karma and other dimensions of reality.

Although many millions of people across the world think religion and religious beliefs are all we need to give us spiritual fulfilment, religion, unfortunately, is not always the answer. Not because of its intrinsic messages - because at their core all religions are about love, tolerance and compassion - but because history has shown us that mankind has chosen instead to use the power of religion to spread a message of division rather than unification and the mistaken belief that wisdom can be imparted only through a man-made hierarchy of religious leaders. This is egotistical behaviour at its worst.

Having a set of beliefs that you regard as 'absolute truth' does not make you spiritual. Being spiritual is to do with your state or level of consciousness because it is your level of consciousness that determines how you conduct yourself and interact with others. And to fully lead a more spiritual life a sense of unification is essential.

As we shall see in Part Two of this book, to move forward through each soul level requires you to have the courage to disentangle yourself from all your material attachments and to stop labelling things so that you feel in control of them. The goal is to stop seeing the world as filled with separate objects, but to start appreciating how it is all connected. For example, when you contemplate the wonders of nature, try to appreciate it without trying to name everything or capturing it in a way that you can categorise it and put a label on it. This is because by trying to label something with a specific name means we are giving our concentration to the naming process to satisfy our egoistic need for control. Instead, you must learn to just let it 'be' and simply acknowledge it for what is *is* - what some spiritual traditions call its, "*is-ness*". Because only then are you starting to see things without any form of judgement rather than trying to own it.

Imagine for a moment walking through a beautiful forest where you are surrounded by an abundance of flowers and wildlife. If you choose to look at every tree, shrub, plant, flower and animal and try and remember its name or dictionary definition you are blocking out that part of you that is open to purely appreciating the forest for what it is as a holistic whole. When our minds are busy with naming things it becomes an academic exercise and blocks our subconscious from simply being aware of beauty without judgement. The simple technique of using just 'awareness' to appreciate things, in contrast, is to start pushing open the doorway into the spiritual realms.

The time has come therefore, to take off your metaphorical blindfold so that you can see the world with new eyes as an interconnected continuum. The time has come to replace intellectual knowledge with intuitive 'heart' wisdom and to become the observer rather than the one the ego controls. Once we have learned to master the ego then we can turn our attention to learning another extremely important spiritual lesson. We now need to understand and acknowledge the 'Law of Karma'.

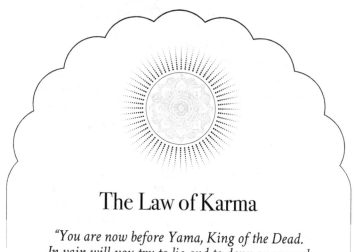

The Law of Karma

*"You are now before Yama, King of the Dead.
In vain will you try to lie and to deny or conceal
the evil deeds you have done. The judge holds up
before you the shining mirror of Karma wherein
all your deeds are reflected. The mirror in which
Yama seems to read your past is your own memory
and also his judgement is your own. It is you
yourself who pronounce your own judgement
which in its turn determines your next birth".*
(Translation from 'The Tibetan Book of the Dead')

It would be impossible to write a book about the
journey of the soul and leave out the 'Law of
Karma' because karma is absolutely fundamental
if we truly wish to understand our life's purpose.
Karma is a much-misunderstood concept, and
although it would take another whole book to
explain it in its entirety, it is essential to cover the
basics of this subject in order to fully understand
what follows.

The standard modern dictionary definition of
'karma' defines it as:

*"The force generated by a person's actions that is believed
in Hinduism and Buddhism to influence their destiny".*
(*"The New Penguin English Dictionary"*)

Another similar definition states that: *"Karma (a Sanskrit word meaning 'action') is a law of cause and effect whereby virtuous actions result in happiness in the future (of this lifetime or a future lifetime) and unvirtuous actions result in suffering. In common English parlance karma has come to mean fate".*
(Professor Donald Lopez)

These definitions are useful, but tend to over-simplify the complexity of karma - possibly because the concept of the law of karma has been deeply embedded in the spiritual wisdom of the East for many centuries and contains many subtle intricacies and nuances that western dictionary definitions often miss.

If we are seeking the most high level or simple explanation of what karma really means it could be summed up as a spiritual law that binds us to experiencing human life by requiring us to go through many incarnations, but even this definition is too limiting in scope.

Probably, the most important thing to understand about karma is that it is not something that is 'out there' - separate from us - that is influencing our life. It is actually something that is already *within* us. In essence it is we who create our own karma. This point is crucial to understand. In other words karma is not created by the people who are around us, or by the society we live within, or any other external influence. We are all totally responsible for our own karma.

We create our own karma by our internal thoughts, feelings, emotions and actions because all of these things contain 'energy' and we live in a universe composed primarily of energy. The universe, or spiritual realms to be more precise, is affected by all fluctuations in the universal quantum energy field and can detect or 'pick up', like a radio signal, the emotions that precede every pulse of energy. Let's try and put this concept into easier terms to make it more understandable.

Because the universe is composed of energy and all thoughts and emotions are also composed of energy, it means that every thought or action we create has a small but direct influence on the universe. And, because the spiritual realms exist in a form of purity, they cannot be contaminated by negative energies - which means that any negative actions or thoughts that we generate are reflected back on us as individuals. Sometimes negative actions or thoughts are simply referred to as 'bad' karma whilst positive or loving thoughts are referred to as 'good' karma. This implies, in simple terms, that bad karma affects us negatively and good karma affects us positively which is essentially true, although 'good' and 'bad' are highly subjective terms. It would be more accurate to think of karma in a different way. It is more like a constant energy interaction that continues throughout our entire life due to our subconscious telepathic connection to the spirit world. In other words, whether we are consciously aware of it or not, our every thought transmits an energetic pulse back and forth between our mind and the universe. That energetic pulse of thought contains intentions that might be positive (a loving or compassionate thought) or negative (an angry or revengeful thought) and all these accumulated thoughts are 'stored' in an energetic library that the ancients called the 'Akashic Records'.

But behind this universal truth there is something that it is very important to understand. The universe always remains 'neutral'. The universe is not human and it does not share human beliefs about what is 'right' or what is 'wrong'. Similarly, it does not recognise human notions of prejudice or judgement or what is deemed to be 'illegal' or 'legal'. In short, the universe is incapable of passing any sort of judgement one way or the other. The universe cannot react to what we think or do because it does not speak our language. It reacts only to subtle fluctuations in energy. This is how it communicates with itself and with us. So we must be careful with our words here. It is better to substitute in our minds the word, 'right' with 'in accordance and alignment with the motives of our higher self' and the word 'wrong' with '*not* in accordance or alignment with the motives of our higher self'. With these words the distinctions become much clearer.

What this means is that the universe can never punish us or reward us in the literal sense, as many people seem to believe. It is we - not the universe - who are constantly having an affect on our own karma because of the things we think about and the things that we do. Every thought is a 'thing' that creates energy and the nature of the thought reflects back on us and affects us in ways we can barely perceive. Our karma is therefore defined not by some random external agency, but rather by who we are, what we think, what we do and, more especially, what motives lie behind our thoughts and actions.

When we apply this philosophy to our spiritual path from ignorance to enlightenment we begin to understand how karma affects our progression on the path. If our thoughts and actions are kind, loving, pure, compassionate and not driven by egoistic desires then we are generating 'good' karma for ourselves (i.e. good energy). If, alternatively, our thoughts and actions are based on egoic motives of greed, revenge, selfishness and self-satisfaction this generates 'bad' karma and thus bad energy. But there is no external 'judge' or 'god' that is dishing out karmic judgement on us. Our karma is only ever determined by ourselves.

So, if we want to progress on our spiritual path by constantly generating good karma this can unquestionably be achieved by maintaining our focus on the quality of our thoughts and actions. Easy to say, for sure - but not always easy to do! None of us are perfect and we all share human failings. This means however, that we can never blame someone else for causing us either good karma or bad karma because we are always the only one in control of our own thoughts. And, because we are the only person solely responsible for our own thoughts then, by definition, it is only we that can determine our own karma. In effect we are defendant, prosecutor, judge and jury all rolled into one.

In order to control our own thoughts in a positive way - and in order to achieve good karma it is essential that we first learn to communicate with our own subconscious mind. The subconscious is what controls our thoughts and emotions and thus our subsequent actions. This means that the 'conscious mind', which is mostly controlled by the ego, needs to be first tamed, mastered and overcome in order to allow us to connect unimpeded to the subconscious. It is all about understanding and comprehending that our 'true self' is mostly held captive by the ego. In order to connect to our true self therefore requires us to set the subconscious free from its cunning and manipulative 'master'.

The other extremely important truth that needs to be grasped in this context is that all of our past life akashic records can be accessed through the subconscious. It is where all the wisdom we have accumulated through countless previous lives is stored. The ego however, which resides only in the conscious mind, lacks this profound wisdom. Everything the ego thinks it 'knows' has been learned only in this current lifetime and is therefore biased, flawed and very limited.

To fully understand karmic law requires an appreciation of these truths. The ideal situation is to be able to focus enough on your own spiritual development in order to recognise when the ego is trying to influence your thoughts and actions and also to recognise when the internal wisdom gained through your previous lives is being given to you from your subconscious. It is, in essence, simply a matter of choice as to which 'voice' you choose to listen to. Are you going to believe the ego-based Earth Plane voice in your head that tries to tell you how to act and think? Or are you going to learn how to ignore the ego and access your true inner self by tapping into the subconscious through meditation or other spiritual techniques? It is always down to your own personal choice.

When we take mastery of our ego and get in touch with our true inner selves then we are halfway to understanding what karma really means. But there is still more work to do. Our spiritual journey of the soul through many incarnations is intrinsically and inextricably bound up with our karma and we cannot therefore separate the two elements of existence from each other. Our behaviours in previous lives have determined our karmic record through all the consequences of our actions through time - which we might tend to label 'good' and 'bad' (although, as previously stated, there is no judgement of good and bad in the spiritual sense). And, what this means is, although we can change our own future by the thoughts and actions we manifest in the days to come, we cannot turn the clock back and change our past lives, thoughts and deeds.

But what we *can* do is learn from them!

To face up to our thoughts and deeds from our past lives takes a lot of courage. Most of us are simply unwilling to re-open such a can of worms because it is too painful. Many of us will have been 'sinners' rather than 'saints' in our previous lives and painful memories are often too difficult to deal with. But if we do find the courage to face up to all the wrong or bad decisions we made in our previous lives - or indeed this life - as well as the consequences we inflicted on others, then we are learning something of profound significance from these revelations and the rewards are many.

To know and accept the things we have done wrong in the past means facing up to some harsh truths and re-witnessing things we would rather forget about. But, if we find the humility to fully acknowledge the mistakes we have made - and thus gain the wisdom to change ourselves in this life - then we are not just healing our soul; we are also truly taking control of our own karma.

Karmic law is therefore central to the concept of the 'Soul Contract', the work we do in our Soul Group between lives, the 'Life Review' we all have to go through after transition with our spirit guides and our own personal freedom of choice.

As stated previously, the Earth Plane is our classroom where we have to learn to navigate our life by overcoming many challenges and obstacles. This is not easy to do because we are all creatures of emotion. We get angry and frustrated, we lose our temper, we get into arguments and disagreements and we have to learn the hard way how to deal with difficult relationships. There is an old saying that, *"where there is drama there is karma"* and this phrase nicely sums up what karma is all about.

Universal law is actually very simple. We are born as pure souls from Source and we return as pure souls to Source. Only pure souls can be accepted back into Source or 'Nirvana' as it is called in the East. Buddhists believe that all human lives are 'suffering' which may sound extreme to western ears. But the actual words do not matter - it is the concept that matters. What the Buddhists mean by the word 'suffering' is that all our incarnations are 'learning journeys'. We return time and again to learn lessons and gain wisdom. We grow from ignorance to enlightenment. These life journeys are often painful because we have to learn to face the worst - and best - of ourselves and the human condition.

We have to learn how to navigate through fear, loss, poverty, pain, sorrow, helplessness and grief. And we also have to experience joy, contentment, gratitude, love and bliss. In some lives we are the aggressor and in other lives we are the victim. We need to experience both extremes if we are to truly learn deep universal lessons. In other words, it is not until we have learned that the consequences of our thoughts, actions, feelings and intentions affect our karmic progression that will we start to mature spiritually.

When we fully acknowledge that we, and we alone, are responsible for how many more challenging lifetimes we have to endure - and accept that the way we think and act *now* will determine our ultimate destiny - then we can set our intentions on how we should live, how we should treat others and how we should act in order to be accepted back into Source as a purified soul.

And the best place to start is through unconditional love. This means learning to love ourselves by first acknowledging and then forgiving ourselves for everything we have previously done wrong. Then we need to forgive those who have 'wronged us' and then unconditionally spread love and forgiveness to everyone around us - whatever their circumstances or issues. If there is one 'golden key' to accelerating our progress on our own personal soul journey and paying off our 'karmic debts' it is this. But let's be very clear at this point that even this commonly used term 'karmic debt' is inaccurate, because it is a Buddhist religious term rather than a spiritual term. In the spirit world of unconditional love there is no such concept of there being any debt to pay. There are only more lessons to be learned.

Before we turn this golden key and unlock the future we desire, there is one more very important concept that needs to be understood that goes hand in glove with the law of karma. It is the law of 'intention'. Because it is not just the *actions* we take that affect our karma, it is also about the *intentions* that precede our actions that are of critical importance.

The Law of Intention

To truly understand the concept of 'Soul Evolution' requires an understanding of what the word 'Intention' means in the spiritual context.

The Spirit world does not judge your actions in the way that actions are judged in the human context. The Spirit world simply observes our actions but does not pass judgement. In a similar way, our definitions of 'right' and 'wrong', 'good' or 'bad', 'true' and 'untrue', 'just' and 'unjust' are not relevant in the Spirit world because we place our own human definitions on these words and they can have different meanings depending on culture, beliefs, language, societal norms and expectations - as well as the time period when these words were first used. For example, the ideas of what constitutes 'just' and 'unjust' would have different connotations in medieval times compared to now.

What is really of paramount interest in the spirit world is the *intention* behind every action, rather than the action itself. And this distinction is critical. Although intention is also *not judged* it is something that we are ultimately held accountable for in the karmic sense because we have responsibility and accountability for our intentions.

A few simple examples can help us to grasp this important concept.

Let's start with a scenario that will be relevant to all parents of young children or teenagers living in today's complex world. Since the mid nineteen eighties mobile phone technology, lightweight portable laptops and other digital devices have changed our world immeasurably. Children today have been born into a world dominated by mobile devices and social media and almost every child in the 'civilized' world desperately awaits the day they can own their own mobile phone. This puts parents under enormous pressure because of the associated risks that come with the power of social media and the internet.

Once children own their own phone most parents tend to restrict screen time because they love their children and want to limit their exposure to reliance on technology. Parents' know instinctively that time reading books, telling stories, playing games and social interaction are all critical components of child development and that playing on mobile phones should be just one part of the day's routines. But mobile phones are addictive and when parent's say, 'Okay, time's up. Turn the phone off now', many children go into tantrums and meltdown. I have personally witnessed this many times.

The point being made though, is all about *intention*. If a parent removes a child's mobile phone and the child reacts with anger or hostility saying "it's not fair", or similar words, the child may well feel the parent is being cruel or unkind. But from the parent's viewpoint, restricting mobile phone time is about love for the child and wanting to prevent the phone time from becoming an addictive behaviour. From the child's perspective the parent is being unkind. But the parent's actual intention is one motivated by love and caring.

If we turn this example around, another scenario is possible. An older child, let's say mid-teens for example, may well become obsessive about their mobile phone usage and some parents tend to discipline their offspring by using the threat of taking away the phone in the event of 'bad' or 'unacceptable' behaviour. In this scenario removing the phone from the teenager is effectively a punishment. In this case the intention has shifted from the loving and caring intention applied to the younger child to a punishment action towards the older child. In the first example the intention was loving. In the second example, although still loving in the wider context, the intention was punishment. This might appear to be a trivial distinction but in spiritual terms this distinction is of paramount importance. This is because it is our intentions that determine what is held in our karmic records more than the action that follows the intention.

An extreme example of this would be the holocaust in the second world war. On the material Earth Plane the Nazi's who committed genocide against the Jews were held accountable by the forces of law for physically causing death and suffering. In the spirit world however, the perpetrators are held karmically accountable for their *'intention to harm'* rather than the 'action of harming' that followed.

Because this is such an important topic let's explore another much less extreme example.

Have you ever had the experience of agonising over a Birthday or Christmas gift for a relative or friend and not known what to buy them? In the end you chose something you hoped they would really like, only to discover later that it was something they didn't like at all? I think most of us have experienced this situation or something very similar. You might have chosen a painting or picture that you would love to have put on your own wall, but then later discover it is in a style that the recipient finds distasteful. Maybe you have bought flowers for someone who has an allergy to flowers or a box of chocolates for someone who has just started a new diet?

My parents like to remind me about my third birthday when my uncle bought me a tin drum and drumsticks. Apparently, I absolutely loved this wonderful gift, but it took years for my long-suffering parents to forgive him as I used to play it loudly and relentlessly day and night! At the time my parents reacted by blaming my uncle for not checking with them first that a tin drum would be an acceptable gift. In other words, my parents made a judgement that the action on his part was 'wrong' and he, in turn, regretted the decision. I, of course, was blissfully happy.

The point here though, is that the Spirit world does not in any way make a judgement about this being a 'wrong' or 'right' action or a 'good' or 'bad' action. Spiritually, the *action* of giving me a tin drum is irrelevant, but the *intention* is extremely relevant. The intention in this case was pure, thoughtful and kind. If my uncle had been trying to be devious or spiteful his intention might have been to make my parents suffer by the incessant sound of a child playing a drum badly - but that was not the case. Only if the *intention* had been to deliberately make someone suffer would there be karmic consequences.

So, the key point here is that when we are talking about the spiritual context of the way we conduct ourselves on our spiritual path, which has 'karmic consequences', it is all about *intention* rather than *outcome*. And the spirit world is making no judgement about whether the action is good or bad or even whether the intention was good or bad. Karma is not dished out by watchful spiritual 'spies'. Our karma is determined only by our own intentions. We are both the accused, the judge and the jury all in one.

This might seem like a small or largely irrelevant distinction, but it is crucially important if we want to understand the way the spirit world functions and operates. Almost every single thought we have during our lives has an 'intention' behind it that later manifests as an 'action' i.e. we decide to go for a walk (intention) and then we actually go for a walk (action).

Whatever the outcome of our intention becomes, good or bad, is therefore of little consequence in the spiritual realms. Instead, it is the subliminal intentions behind every action that determines our progression on our spiritual path. In other words it is the 'thought motive' behind the action that is critical. In short, 'it's the thought that counts!'

What lesson can we, and should we, learn from this?

During our physical existence on this planet our fellow human beings will constantly be judging our every action and probably commenting on them too. Some might approve of our actions while others strongly disapprove of our actions depending on their personal motives, biases and viewpoints. But from the spiritual viewpoint other people's views of your actions on the Earth Plane are totally irrelevant. Spirit is only interested in your *intentions* in a non-judgemental way.

If you make a 'wrong decision' and people suffer, or you take an action that you later regret, as long as your intention at the time was genuine, pure and intended to do good rather than harm then you have nothing to fear. Spirit always perceives the *intentions* behind your actions - and this is all that matters. This is what is recorded in your 'karmic record' and this is one of the key determinants of your ongoing soul progress on your spiritual path. But let's be clear here. Your karmic record is not like a school report of good and bad behaviour written by your teachers. Your spiritual guides are not recording your intentions and actions in some kind of spiritual diary. Your personal karmic record, or diary, is something that you alone own and carry with you through all your incarnations. You are in effect, writing your own report every day and thus determining your own spiritual progression. You alone are master of your own destiny, so be careful if you are blaming anyone else for your situation or predicament on your journey. The responsibility will always remain yours and yours alone and blaming others for your circumstances is pointless.

In short, if your intentions are always heart-centred, loving and caring then you are doing everything Spirit requires of you. And even if the outcomes seem to sometimes go wrong on the 'Earth Plane' they will be always be considered 'right' on the spiritual plane.

Looking into the Mirror

"This being human is a guest house.
Every morning a new arrival. A joy,
a depression, a meanness, some momentary
awareness comes as an unexpected visitor.
Welcome and entertain them all!"
Rumi

Now that we have learned about the way the spiritual realms work in terms of the Law of Intention, karmic law, the cycles of incarnations, life between lives, relationships, the challenges of mastering the ego and our journey on the soul's path, we are finally prepared for the next step on our adventure.

All the information imparted so far has served to set the scene for what is to follow. The next section of this book, which will bring us right down to earth again with a bump, is all about the *here and now* - the everyday harsh reality of living within a human body on a constantly changing planet. It is about the daily stresses of making a living with all the challenges we all have to face in a tough and competitive world.

But now, I hope, you are much better equipped to face these challenges with a much greater depth of knowledge than before. And Part Two of this book will attempt to provide all the answers to your deepest questions about who you really are and why you are here.

However, Part Two comes with a gentle advance warning: It demands an open and receptive mind to face up to certain truths about ourselves and sometimes looking 'into the mirror' can be a little bit scary because it is often much easier to hide from the truth than face up to it head on. And, as we now know, the ego does not like to be criticised!

For those brave enough to look into the mirror however, the answers are all there waiting to be revealed. You may now know and accept that you are a beautiful and immortal soul on a very important journey, but you might still be asking questions like, "But where exactly am I on my journey?"; "How far have I already travelled and how many lives have I already been through?"; "What is likely to happen to me next on this journey?"; "What can I do to get to my final destination more quickly?" etcetera. These are all very valid and important questions because our own spiritual journey really is the most important thing in our entire lives. Everything else is just peripheral. And when we finally come to realise this truth, whether it be during life number one or life number one thousand, or somewhere in-between, then we cannot help but want to access the map that defines our own personal journey from start to finish.

The answers to these deep questions, and access to the map of your own spiritual journey, can all be found in Part Two of this book which I hope you are going to enjoy reading.

Vibration, Frequencies
and Energies

B efore examining the seven stages of the soul in
detail it is important to briefly raise the subject
of what might be termed 'spiritual energy' because
this concept is central to any discussion of soul
development and progress on our life path and
journey.

As any quantum physicist knows, at the heart of
everything in the entire universe there is only one
fundamental primordial essence and that is energy.
So-called 'matter' is an illusion. We, and everything
that exists, are merely energy at the quantum level
of reality. Every tree, table, car, planet or person is
nothing more than energy assembled into a 'thing'
that our eyes perceive as solid matter but in truth
is no more than a constantly fluctuating vibration
of energy. The lower the vibration then the more
dense it appears in terms of physicality or material
existence. The higher the vibration the more
immaterial 'it' becomes.

This fundamental truth has been known by all the
great spiritual traditions for centuries and has only
relatively recently been acknowledged in totality
by the scientific community. Science continued to

assume for the last few hundred years that there had to be some kind of minute building block of matter at the heart of the atom and were hugely frustrated that as the technology improved and enabled the atom to be split down further and further there was nothing that constituted matter at all - just a microscopic vibration that held everything together.

But this is not a book about quantum physics. It is about this fundamental truth that all matter is composed of energy that vibrates at specific frequencies in order to give us this experience we call life.

Whatever we choose to call this energy 'Chi', 'Prana' or 'The Force' (as it is called in the Star Wars films), the actual word does not really matter. Without these constantly vibrating frequencies we would be unable to exist or to manifest that existence as a living, breathing immortal soul.

So why is this concept so important to understand? It is because as we learn to accept and acknowledge that we are all vibrational entities we slowly start to become more consciously aware of those energies and frequencies that are operational within our own bodies. And, as we start to lead a more spiritual life we start to become more attuned with those frequencies that are vibrating within us and the subtleties and nuances of how they change over time. Those who regularly meditate or practice mindfulness know these feelings well and start to build an inner sense of their own energy levels and how vibrational frequencies act in relation to their physical and mental health.

In traditional Western medical practice illness is something caused by an external agency and our bodies are viewed in a similar way as a car mechanic views a car. If a part of the car is not working as it should, you either remove it or replace it, as a surgeon would surgically remove a cancerous tumour or replace a broken joint with a synthetic prosthetic. And if you are not feeling good then you are likely to be prescribed a synthetic drug to combat your 'condition'.

In the East the whole concept of health and disease is viewed very differently. In Eastern tradition all illness starts from an energy blockage; because if Chi or Prana are somehow being blocked from flowing naturally then illness will surely follow and manifest as a physical issue. So to fix the health problem requires removing the energy blockage through techniques like acupuncture and reiki. In the context of Part Two of this book it is important to recognise this important distinction.

Our spirit guides tell us that our 'vibrational health' is intrinsically connected to the way we feel, think, behave and act. And, as we progress on our journey through many lives and slowly move from Level One to Level Seven on our soul path so our level of vibration shifts from 'low vibration' existence as a Level One soul to a 'high vibration' existence by the time we reach Level Seven. This is a critically important point to understand. Low vibration thinking and action leads to prejudice, discrimination, segregation, conflict, suffering and war. High vibration thinking leads to unconditional love, compassion, forgiveness, gratitude, connection, humility and empathy.

But, that being said, low vibration actions are not necessarily 'bad' in the spiritual context just as high vibration actions are not necessarily 'good'. Both are equally necessary to be experienced on our soul journey because both ends of the spectrum need to be lived and acknowledged before we can move on up the ascension ladder towards Source. Every single one of us started our journey at Stage One and we must never forget that. To truly integrate this wisdom into our life we must all be prepared to lose the influence our ego has over us so that there is no judgement of superiority or inferiority.

As we will come to understand in Part Two, low vibration Level One souls and high vibration Level Seven souls must both be unconditionally accepted as beautiful souls following their own path. Both deserve love, acceptance and respect whatever stage they are at on their journey. For ultimately, we all arrive at the same place where we are welcomed as equals regardless of the route we have chosen to take and the time it has taken for us to arrive.

PART TWO

*"We are not human beings
having a spiritual experience;
we are spiritual beings
having a human experience".*
Tielhard de Chardin

The Soul's Journey
on the Earth Plane
(The Seven Stages)

*"You have been alive since the beginning of time,
in a gorgeous unbroken continuum, moving back and
forth between earth and the 'other side' many times.
You have lived on earth in many different bodies,
during many different eras in many different parts
of the world under many different circumstances for
your own carefully chosen purpose, depending on the
goals and needs of your spirit's progress".
("Life on the Other Side" by Sylvia Brown)*

O ver the years, when I have given talks about
the journey of the soul, there is very often a
question asked by someone in the audience that
is usually shared by many others. The question is
framed something like this:

*"I know and I understand that I am an immortal soul
on a journey - but what I'm not sure of is where exactly
I am on that journey. Am I at the start, the middle or
near the end?"*

This a good question because it is not always easy to
ascertain where we are on the long and sometimes

difficult path to spiritual enlightenment and soul maturity. It is difficult to self-assess or self-analyse simply because we cannot make a dispassionate and independent judgement on a life we are in the midst of living! There are many souls who assume they are very enlightened and must have almost repaid all their karmic debts from previous lives - while other, more humble souls, feel they are just starting out. The first response I usually give to this question is, "You are exactly where you are meant to be!" which, whilst true, is not always the most useful or satisfactory answer.

Part Two of this book, however, serves to address this specific question in a much more detailed and comprehensive way by examining each of the seven stages of the soul's journey on the Earth Plane in considerable depth. I hope the information that follows, which has come directly from the spiritual realms and is a gift for all of us to share, provides the answers that you, dear reader, are seeking.

It should be mentioned at this point that before we start examining each of the seven stages of the soul in depth, that using this 'seven step model' is just one of many different ways of explaining - or thinking about - our soul's journey through many thousands of lifetimes. For some readers it might be helpful to think of this progression in another conceptual way to aid our understanding. For example, another term for the seven stages could be 'Soul Ages' in which we equate our progress on our journey to the stages of maturity in one human life. So we might call a Stage One soul a 'Baby Soul' representing a soul in the very earliest stage of its development. Using this scenario we could say a Stage Two soul is an 'Infant Soul', a Stage Three soul a 'Youth Soul', a Stage Four soul a 'Teenage Soul', a Stage Five soul an 'Adult Soul', a Stage Six soul a 'Mature Soul' and a Stage Seven Soul an 'Old Soul'. It doesn't really matter how we prefer to label the seven stages because it is just a useful way of conceptualising how the soul evolves from immaturity to maturity. And of course, it should always be remembered that the boundaries that we cross between each stage or soul age is never a hard or clear cut boundary but rather a steady transition.

All stories start at the beginning and our journey on the 'Soul's path' also needs to start at the beginning. Every soul is on this journey and every soul must therefore take the first tentative steps on the path that stretches forward into the unknown. This takes courage and determination because we don't yet know what we are going to encounter on this path. We are apprehensive because there may be unseen dangers around every corner. There might be irresistible temptations that draw us away from the path. There might be people we meet who try to influence us and try to persuade us that we are on the 'wrong path'. We might lose our way in the darkness or in confusion and temporarily wander off the path. Or we might lose our courage and be tempted to turn around and retrace our steps as it has become too scary to keep moving forward. All these things are likely to happen and, in reality, probably have happened in our past and are likely to happen again.

If the path was easy to navigate and we were able to walk effortlessly from the start to the finish as though we were on a gentle walking holiday it may well be a pleasurable experience. But that is all it would be. Simply, a pleasurable experience! But just imagine walking a thousand 'easy paths' or even ten thousand. Eventually the monotony would become interminably boring and we would seek distractions or new experiences just to entertain us or to relieve the boredom.

The path of life that stretches out in front of each of you right now - today - is not like any other path you may have traversed for a very important reason. It is not a 'random' path but something that is completely the opposite of random. It is a path that has been uniquely designed for you - and you alone.

Your unique path was designed for you by the spirit world before you were even born. It has been very carefully constructed with precision and accuracy and planned in detail - even though, at all times, we always have the freedom to exercise our free will as we please and change our route. Like a surgeon planning for a complex operation or a wellness trainer designing the perfect customised exercise regime and nutrition plan, our spirit guides have meticulously prepared our 'life path' for us and then they watch us with pride as we take every small step - whichever 'direction' we choose to take. But this life path planning was also something that we ourselves played a major part in as explained briefly in the 'Many Precious Lives' section of this book in Part One. Not only do we have the opportunity to review our previous life with our spiritual teachers and guides when we are between lives, but we also play an extremely active part in planning our next life with our soul group and our guides. In other words we actually decide on the lessons we need to learn and the challenges we need to face up to and overcome. We are therefore instrumental in planning our own next life.

But why? Why should our spirit guides have to spend their precious time constructing a soul path just for us? And why would they place so many obstacles in our way and make it so hard for us to stay on the path?

The answer is two-fold. Firstly, our spirit guides exist in order to support us and help us; so, they are totally focused on assisting us on our journey. They are not 'wasting their time' because this is exactly how they choose to spend their time! In a sense, getting us to complete our life path is *their* mission. And secondly, planet Earth is our primary training ground. Every obstacle we face up to, every difficult situation we resolve and every difficult person we deal with, is part of OUR mission. This means that every single obstacle or challenge that awaits us on our path is there for a reason. Our mission in life is to learn - and every obstacle or challenge we face up to, and learn from, is a lesson completed.

Some of these challenges are deliberately extremely tough and sometimes we succeed and sometimes we fail. Overcoming an obstacle or challenge successfully is a priceless lesson learned. And that, in very simple terms, is exactly what we are here for. But even when we 'fail' at a task time and again, this is never considered permanent failure. If we choose to persevere and use every means at our disposal to get through the tough times or tough situations until we eventually break through, then another important lesson has been learned. It is like learning to ride a bike or learning to swim for the first time. Yes - we can give up and stop trying. Or we can keep going and persevere until both these skills have been mastered.

And, essentially, that is what our lives are all about - learning to face up to every challenge we encounter on our soul journey.

In our life we must be prepared to experience things like wars, droughts, famines, bereavement, loss, illness, hurt, rejection, sadness, uncertainty, fear, hopelessness, despair, apathy, denial and many more trials. Life is never - or very rarely - easy. At some point or other on our soul's journey this reality often comes as a kind of internal revelation or burst of awareness or insight. Suddenly we wake up and realise that our life really does have a definite purpose and that purpose is to overcome all the challenges that come our way. Because each and every challenge overcome is a lesson learned. And each lesson learned is a step closer to entering the next level or stage on our soul's journey.

If we continually fail to meet our challenges head-on during our journey and prefer to stay in some sort of 'safe zone' that is still okay. In the spirit world this will never constitute failure, because the spirit world is infinitely patient. We have to find our own way in our own time. There is never any pressure from the universe.

So, we always have freedom of choice while on our path. We have the choice to continue moving forward and facing up to our difficult challenges or we can retreat and take a few steps backward. Alternatively, we can just 'stay put' and pause on our journey and take some time out for personal reflection. The choice is always ours.

Now that we understand the reasons we are here and the importance of our soul journey, the time has come to find out where we are on our own very individual and specific path and what the future is likely to hold for us. It is time to examine in detail the seven stages of the soul.

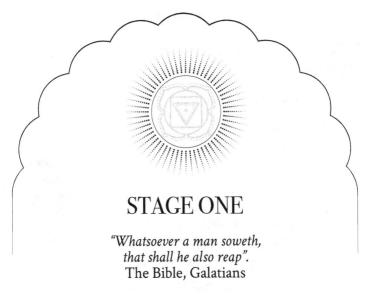

STAGE ONE

"Whatsoever a man soweth,
that shall he also reap".
The Bible, Galatians

CHAKRA: ONE (EARTH)

Sanskrit Name - 'Muladhara'
Location - Base of the spine
Colour - Red
Common Name - 'Root' or 'Base' chakra
Characteristics - The focus is on solid earthly
and tangible things such as the physical body and
satisfying the needs of the ego, physical survival,
self-preservation, physical matter, material
objects, ambition, money, possessions, security,
competition, scepticism and hard science.

Tarot Card: 'The Fool'

The first card of the Tarot, traditionally card number
'0', is 'The Fool'. It represents innocence but also
ignorance. The Fool, at the very start of his journey, is
an 'unenlightened soul' that is simply accepting life as it
is without questioning anything. The Fool at this stage
is ruled totally by 'ego' and has no conception of his
or her own immortal soul or spiritual destiny. Unless

something changes his - or her - life will continue in blissful ignorance.

Hero's Journey: 'Prelude to Adventure'

The Hero is at the threshold of an exciting journey but not yet aware that the journey is about to begin. The 'Call to Adventure' is imminent but at this point in time the Hero is still enjoying the comforts and certainties of home. Everything is continuing as 'normal' and is therefore reassuring and comfortable. There is no sense of 'change in the air' or danger lurking ahead. The Hero is comfortable that all is well and life is proceeding much as it always has done.

Let's make something very clear, right at the outset, so there is no misunderstanding.

There is no shame at all in being a beautiful and unique soul at the start of your soul's journey on the path. Without any exception, each and every one of us has to start at the beginning. Whether we call it 'Stage One', 'Level One' or 'Step One' it does not matter. We are all exactly where we are *meant to be,* and there is nothing we can personally do to change that - except perhaps, to have an aspiration to move forward as best we can. Most of us go through many lives, perhaps thousands, as 'Stage One' souls until the time we are ready to take another huge step into the challenges and joys of 'Stage Two'.

Some of the most intelligent and highly qualified and respected people in the world will fall into this category so we need to be absolutely clear that our level of intelligence or intellectual knowledge, capabilities and experience has no bearing on our

Soul Level which some might find surprising. In other words, we may have led our current life having achieved many great accomplishments, academically or physically, and received great acclaim and recognition. We may be rich and successful and undoubtedly this is to be admired and applauded. This is deemed to be success on the Earth Plane and rightly so. But it has no bearing on our soul level or soul maturity as we shall see in the coming pages.

Many souls at this early stage of their journey can outwardly appear to be 'model' citizens and worthy of much respect and admiration. We are all the products of the society in which we grew up and many of us, but certainly not all of us, have had the benefits of loving parents and a reasonable education. Even those who have had early life struggles and may have been orphaned or suffered a number of deprivations have often worked even harder than most to achieve a better life for themselves by overcoming all the obstacles on their path.

When we were young, we usually accepted what our parents and peers taught us about life. And when our schools, colleges and universities endorsed these 'truths' they became part of our philosophy of life. In other words, we were all given a personal, but mostly unwritten, 'book of rules' that we have used throughout our life as our predominant guiding principles as we have matured and flourished. These are the unwritten moral and ethical rules that we choose to abide by and are used within the framework that we live within. They are, in essence, the 'core beliefs' that give us stability and reassurance and provide the bedrock that we need to keep us grounded and able to function in a tough competitive world.

Some of these societal 'norms' have become so entrenched into our psyche that we now take most of them for granted. And many of these norms are evidenced by our real-life experiences. For example, we are taught at a young age that life is about competition and we sometimes have to fight for our share of the 'pie'. We are told by careers advisors that we need to study hard to become qualified so that we can find our niche in work and in society. We are taught that having money is critical to our success in life and being poor is to be avoided at all costs. We are bombarded with consumerist media tempting us to buy more and more 'stuff' and so we aspire to acquire more and more essentials that we believe we cannot do without. Job security becomes of paramount concern as does being adequately insured and securely pensioned.

And so, most of us fall into the inevitable trap and, before we know it, we are all on a treadmill that we simply accept as something called 'normal life'. As Stage One souls we often feel blessed to lead what might be called a normal life, because this is the life our parents and our grandparents aspired to and then wished for us. And, in our modern society, this is what we believe to be the measure of our success. But what do we mean by 'normality'? For many people across the world who live in much more difficult circumstances a normal life is something extremely desirable. Sometimes referred to as 'The American Dream' it is something surely worth striving for? We seem to have set up this idealised model of reality to measure how successful - or not successful - we are, so that every single one of us has a specific goal to aspire to. But 'normal' is not really the best description for all Stage One souls because clearly what is normal for some of us, is not the same as other people's normal. It's all relative. But it does give us a useful starting point.

So, with these key factors in mind, how can we best describe 'typical' Stage One souls? Well, firstly, let's make a clear and definitive statement: All souls who are at Stage One are usually *totally unaware* that they are at Stage One. In fact, they probably have no conception of being at any stage at all. And, if a friend or colleague who is a 'higher level' soul ever chose or dared to mention to them that they were a 'Stage One' soul, the higher level soul would simply be mocked and ridiculed. A Stage One soul, by their very nature, doesn't like to be labelled as anything they don't understand. Even if it is a fundamental truth.

Let's start by examining the typical characteristics of typical Stage One souls. Firstly, most Stage One souls, not unsurprisingly, like to have the security of having somewhere to call 'home' - whether it is a house, caravan or castle. They need somewhere they can base or ground themselves like a personal sanctuary to come back to after a hard day at work. Home, so-called 'bricks and mortar' is their security. And, in that home environment, most Stage One souls will at some time start a family and initiate a new generation. A time of joy and, hopefully, contentment.

In today's stressful times, Stage One souls will try to keep abreast of the daily news via TV, newspapers or social media. If they can afford it, most Stage One souls will own a laptop and mobile phone which provide them with their 'lifeline'. They may well be interested in economics and politics and try to keep up with what is going on in the world through online or printed media. Many Stage One souls like to keep themselves active and enjoy leisure time hobbies like golf, fishing, jogging, cycling or watching the sport on TV. Most Stage One souls read the daily newspapers but also enjoy reading novels for relaxation. Most, but not all, Stage One souls are social creatures and enjoy a good social life with friends. Having peer acceptance is very important to them too. They like to be part of the group or part of the team.

Stage One souls are generally good natured but, at times, can be very competitive and don't like being challenged either verbally or physically. And, what they hate most, is feeling out of their depth. But, in general terms, Stage One souls are what we call 'normal people' and there is no shame in that at all. Most, if not all of us, have lived through this type of experience through many lifetimes and probably hugely enjoyed it too.

When we are going through a Stage One life most of us tend to be very opinionated and hold fairly firm beliefs about the world in general and our place in it. We tend to be in touch with our feelings and are able to express our anger very openly when we feel it is necessary. We believe that expressing anger is our personal right and some Stage One souls can even become aggressive if they feel aggrieved, cheated or threatened. Their world-view is often based on the belief that they live in a 'dog-eat-dog world' that is brutally competitive and survival is based on competitive advantage where the best man (or woman) wins.

Some Stage One souls hold religious beliefs and convictions, but the majority tend to be 'agnostic' and have a fairly clinical view of life based on the simple premise that we are born, we live and then we die. It's a simple three stage process. Similarly, the body is broadly viewed as a mechanical organism that sometimes gets ill. When it gets ill then the solution is to go to the doctors, get a diagnosis, pick up a subscription, take the medications that the doctor has recommended then hope that recovery will follow.

Stage One souls are generally tolerant of 'others' whatever their religion, culture, skin colour or sexual orientation might be, but are more likely to hold stronger opinions about these others than the souls in the higher stages of maturity. They prefer to socialise with other Stage One souls - who are like-minded - than souls from other stages, of whom they are slightly suspicious of because they are viewed as somehow 'different'. Many Stage One souls are what might be termed 'bar stool philosophers', which is not a derogatory term in this context, but reflects their tendency to impose their beliefs and world views on anyone that is willing to listen. Most Stage One souls can be very opinionated and not always good at listening or willing to see life from other people's perspective.

Stage One souls can also be recognised by certain other behavioural traits which tend to fall away as they progress on their path to the higher stages.
Stage One souls find it very hard to forgive those who they feel have wronged them in some way. If someone upsets or angers a Stage One soul then the Stage One response is the need for revenge or to incite ongoing conflict rather than finding a more amenable solution. Forgiveness is simply not on the agenda. Similarly Stage One souls can be aggressive, even if only slightly provoked, will not listen to reason and are focused only on getting their own back in some way. They are often confrontational, abusive and willing to get into a fight - verbal or physical - in order to resolve issues. For most Stage One souls, 'an eye for an eye'

is their guiding philosophy and revenge is their idea of obtaining justice.

It has already been stated though, that many Stage One souls can be extremely intelligent and successful in life. In fact, it is perfectly possible for Stage One souls to be anywhere on the spectrum from brain surgeons or university professors to repeat offenders in prison or violent psychopaths. And they are just as likely to be a film or pop star as someone living on the streets. This is because, as previously stated, the stages of soul development are not about occupation, social position or IQ. It is just about an individual's level of spiritual growth and this is the crucial point.

That is why the media likes to create news stories about famous people who display Stage One behaviour. When someone famous falls from grace by being exposed in some way - getting into a fight, getting drunk, being abusive or sexually exploitative etc - it gets a lot of media coverage. That's because we assume a film star or millionaire must somehow be above us in the social hierarchy. But the news story reveals they are just people like the rest of us with the same feelings and the same failings. We are all human.

Sometimes Stage One souls are called 'Baby Souls' because they are at the very start of their spiritual development and, to an extent, can display baby-like behaviour in terms of demanding attention and getting frustrated if they are ignored.

Stage One souls who are violent and abusive, get into fights, upset others and seem drawn to conflict might not be the sort of people with whom we want to be associated. But we should never forget they are still beautiful immortal souls on their own unique learning journey that need to be loved, respected and supported. We may not share their philosophy of life or their over-competitive attitude but we can still encourage them on their journey as best we can. And helping others to move forward on their soul path is something we should all aspire to because when we offer help we are also progressing our own spiritual development. It's a win-win situation.

At Stage One we are generally also caught up in the field of what has been called 'mass consciousness' and often held in the trance of consumerism, subservient to the norms of 'civilised' Society. We are generally good, law abiding citizens, and we work hard and pay our taxes. We tend to believe everything - or the majority of things - that we have learned in life or been taught at school and we like conformity and knowing where we stand. We go to work, come home, watch TV, read the paper, socialise down the pub or on the golf course and form our own opinions and political biases/ persuasions based on what we are exposed to by the media.

Although we may have strong views on some subjects, we tend to only question things that are of personal interest. If there are things we don't understand, but don't directly affect us, we are likely to ignore them. We accept what 'is' and try to navigate it as best we can. Life is tough, and Stage One souls need to be tough in order to survive.

In simple, and high level terms, Stage One souls live in this bubble that most of the world's population recognise and refer to as normality or everyday reality. We buy our food at the supermarket, we go to work, we get angry at what upsets us, we try to put up with things we disagree with, we get anxious about our finances, we try to stay healthy, we do our best to get along with our families and neighbours and we do our best just to survive as best we can.

This sort of thinking often creates an 'Us and Them' mentality which is fairly common for all Level One souls. And the reason for this is all to do with ego which was explored in the first half of this book. The story of the maturity of the soul is all about moving from Stage One of the soul journey through to Stage Seven in small incremental steps and the defining element of soul progress is directly related to the ego. If we were to to sum up this whole book into one sentence that describes what the soul's journey is all about, it would be this:

"The journey of every soul is from the ego-centric way of life to the spiritual-centric way of life".

And it really is as simple as that.

When we are at Stage One our life revolves around our own personal ego. We are totally focused on looking after 'Number One' and we are totally guided by our ego. Only when the ego has been finally conquered can we aspire to reaching Level Seven when 'unity consciousness' replaces 'ego consciousness' and the journey has been completed.

That is why Stage One souls tend to accept their lives as reflecting real life - a struggle to survive in a tough world. There is no space for other realities in this philosophy. Life is what it is. Period. You are either a winner or a loser. That's it. We sometimes hear the term 'panic buying' on the news whenever there is an economic or social crisis and see film of people clearing the shelves in supermarkets pushing and shoving each other as they jostle to fill their trolleys before anyone else can. This competition to get in first often leads to aggression and arguments and is an archetypal Stage One response to any crisis. It is based on the premise that their need is greater than everyone else's which is classic ego-centric behaviour.

Connected to this preoccupation with looking after number one is what can be termed 'fear-based' behaviour. On a sliding scale of 'Behavioural Traits' fear-based behaviours lie at the bottom end of the scale whilst what we might call unconditional love lies at the upper extreme. All other behaviours lie somewhere in between.

As any psychologist or psychotherapist knows well, fear-based behaviours have historically been the root cause of most major global conflicts and wars as well as local battles and skirmishes. It is what divides us from our neighbours and is based on the us and them mentality that has divided mankind from time immemorial. And, sadly, it is just as prevalent today as it was in the past. The war with Iraq, for example, was justified on the fear-based logic that Iraq's weapons of mass destruction needed to be neutralised despite the fact that no such weapons were ever discovered.

Fear-based behaviour is what drives Level One souls to be the first one in the queue for food, petrol or any other commodities. It leads them to believe that they have some kind of superiority or entitlement to have priority over others. Because, to their way of ego-based thinking, they should be the first one to be rescued by the lifeboat at sea or the first one to get treated in a hospital. If you really want to know how to spot a Stage One soul in a crowd, their behaviour will always give them away.

Most Stage One souls are generally obedient within society, although some souls do get involved in crime. Some may take medication, alcohol or drugs to numb themselves from the challenges of harsh reality and they can also feel depressed at times. It is fair to say that many, but not all, Stage One souls live in constant frustration, almost as if in a trance, and may spend many hours staring at a TV screen, mobile phone screen or online games. They tend to look for many forms of distraction to take their mind away from harsh world realities to entertain themselves, whether it be down the pub, on social media or in the gym. Also, although many Stage One souls are concerned by matters such as climate change or global sustainability many others still believe that nature is there to be exploited and animals are there to be eaten. Blaming others for world problems is considered normal behaviour but self-blame is to be avoided at all costs. This is because of the ego.

Another trait of typical Stage One souls is that, in some cases, they can tend to swear a lot in everyday speech. In the context of this book this is not a superior judgement or criticism. It is just how it 'is' and it is more to do with how words are used in the spiritual context. Souls on Stage One of their path believe that words are just 'words'. Period. So, in that sense, swear words are just like any other words and are simply an expression of emotion. But when souls arrive at Stage Five or Six in their soul journey, words have a very different connotation. In the later stages of soul development, as we shall see, words have more than just a literal meaning. Every word has its own 'energy' and that intrinsic energy can be positively or negatively charged. So, as souls develop along the path, there is a natural and often subconscious inclination to use only words that are imbued with positive energy and the tendency to use negatively charged words gradually diminishes.

But let's be clear and realistic about this. Some of our greatest thinkers, philosophers, scientists, artists, inventors and leaders are at this Stage One level on their life path and are exactly where they are supposed to be in terms of their soul evolution. So, if we accept this as a given then the obvious question arises: "What is the difference then between a Stage One soul and a Stage Two soul?" Although there are many differences - as well as similarities - between a Level One soul and a Level Two soul there is one key difference that is paramount and that is all to do with what we call 'Spirituality'.

To make sense of this distinction, however, requires a certain level of generality. People don't like being put in boxes for very valid reasons so any broad-brush generalities are not always helpful. But, in order to clarify the distinction between souls on Stage One of the path, and those on Stage Two of the path, some generalities are inevitable and necessary in order to explain these distinctions. In the 'real world' everyone is different, and it is the same in the spirit world. We all retain our individuality and our personality through hundreds and maybe thousands of incarnations. This is because our individuality and our personality are unique to us. They are the essence of who we are - and this essence is retained whether we are in a physical form living on planet Earth or in a non-physical form in the spirit world. As a human being or as a soul we are still ourselves and always will be.

As we have seen earlier, in general terms a Level One soul is intelligent, rational, scientific, open-minded to a degree but often sceptical about things that cannot be 'proven'. Level One souls like order, logic, full explanations of everything, balanced judgements, rational arguments and solid proof when it comes to things that they are not sure about.

They like to observe the world through the lens that they have been taught to use since they were born and - let's face it - we are all the products of our upbringing and the influence of our parents, our education and our peer group.

Level One souls trust their own senses rather than other people's opinions. What is 'real' to them is what they can see with their eyes, hear with their ears, smell with their nose, taste with their lips and touch with their hands. They are comfortable with things that can be scientifically proven - particularly things that can be accurately measured, deeply analysed and checked in 'double blind', peer-reviewed and scientifically assessed tests. When they see the real data they are happy to accept it as undeniable proof and this protects their credibility in society and their acceptance as someone who is reliable, logical, rational, sceptical and trustworthy. Someone definitely not prone to wasting time on airy-fairy or conspiracy theory type new-age nonsense.

Most people in the Level One stage of development love to use the words, "Prove it..." because if something can be unequivocally or scientifically 'proven' then it must therefore be reliable and this gives the person a sense of superiority because they are now in possession of what they believe to be the truth.

Level One souls in this category can sometimes become slightly obsessed with finding proof about everything they encounter in life and anything that cannot be proven is therefore doubted and labelled as unscientific, unproven and therefore, by definition, unreliable. It must therefore be discarded. Most people at this level find comfort in being with like-minded individuals who share their scientific-sceptical view of the world. They trust these like-minded people because they can indulge in intellectual debates about various scientific theories or new discoveries within their own safety and comfort zones.

If they ever meet someone who they deem to be too spiritual they feel out of their depth and try to avoid conversation rather than listening to these ridiculous, alternative views of the world which, as die-hard sceptics, simply frustrates or annoys them. Words like 'aura', 'chakra', 'angel', 'karma', 'reincarnation', 'spirit guides', 'channelling', 'psychic', 'energy healing' or 'spirit world' are an anathema to Level One souls who regard such terms as at best, unscientific and unproven or at worst ludicrous and 'lunatic fringe'.

Level One souls will always find spiritual concepts difficult to accept because intellectually they can feel affronted to think that their rationality and healthy scepticism is somehow being challenged. But to think like this is actually missing the point. The rational 'scientific method' is one of mankind's greatest achievements and has brought us untold benefits and improvements to our quality of life. There is no shame in wanting to uphold this model of reality because it is proven to be hugely beneficial.

It is just that this is not the 'only' reality - as all spiritually mature souls intuitively recognise.

Trying to scientifically prove or measure things like love, compassion, empathy, altruism or any 'sixth sense' abilities like intuition or extra-sensory perception are essentially a pointless exercise. But it doesn't mean they don't exist.

In the spiritual realms the progress of science is only frowned upon when technology is used to inflict hurt on others or damages the natural environment. In all other respects it is accepted as a natural part of our development as a species. And a healthy scepticism is also, of course, a very valuable attribute.

Today, there are an increasing number of philosophers and scientists who are starting to bridge the gap between science and spirituality. Particularly when the latest findings of quantum physics are exactly aligning with many ancient explanations for how the spiritual and quantum worlds operate. For example, for over a hundred years scientists have been trying to identify the smallest atomic particles, sometimes called the building blocks of matter. And what has been discovered at the very lowest level is that there is no such thing as matter. There are only fluctuations of energy just as mystics, philosophers and seers were telling us two thousand years ago. A Stage One soul does not want to hear this because it challenges the core of their belief system. "*It's not science!*" they protest in indignation.

I once asked a very good friend of mine, a very obvious Stage One soul, what would he think if a UFO landed in his back garden and little green aliens came out and said 'Hello' to him. He thought about this deeply for a few moments with a deep frown on his face and then said very honestly and truthfully; "Well I'd be amazed and shocked. But I still wouldn't believe in them." This is the Stage One archetypal response and a perfect example of how most Stage One souls would think and react.

Although the 'spiritual' element is probably the biggest distinction between a Level One soul and a Level Two soul there are also many other characteristics of Level One souls which are worth elucidating.

The shift out of Stage One into Stage Two cannot be influenced by anything we do, regardless of our wishes or actions. The decision to move us out of Stage One and into Stage Two of our soul journey is made by Spirit alone. As we mature and grow there may well be a time in our life where we feel we have learned all the lessons given to us during Stage One and also feel that we are now ready to face up to the new challenges of Stage Two. But we cannot directly influence that. Our internal feelings will, however, be instantly picked up by our soul guides who will know that we feel ready to progress and may decide to accelerate our development. Generally, though, 'Soul guides' and 'Spirit guides' (the terms can be used interchangeably) do not interfere in our soul journey with one major exception (covered in the next section).

As will be repeated time and again in this book, we are *always* exactly where we are supposed to be - and although we might aspire to move faster this is not how the universe works. If we are a Stage One soul, then we remain a Stage One soul until the universe recognises that the time has come to nudge us gently forward into Stage Two - the next phase of our journey. And the timing of that nudge will always depend on two critical factors - firstly, have we learned everything we are supposed to have learned in Stage One? And, secondly, are we now mentally and spiritually prepared for the challenges of Stage Two?

Leaving the spiritual dimension aside for a moment though, what other broad generalisations can be made about the attributes of Level One souls?

The most important distinction is to do with what we call awareness. Most Stage One souls, but not all, are simply not aware that they are actually following a soul path or soul journey. They are very comfortable in simply accepting they are living beings on planet Earth leading a normal life between birth and death. As they don't tend to believe in the afterlife or the immortality of the soul and believe most spiritual concepts are airy-fairy nonsense, then they have no interest in their own spiritual journey - just their down to earth day to day existence. This is probably the biggest single differentiator between a soul at Stage One of their journey and all the other souls at Stage Two and above.

Stage One of our soul journey is something we all have to experience and endure, sometimes again and again through many lifetimes. It is the essential starting point of our soul evolution and needs to be recognised and acknowledged for what it is. The Earth is a tough training ground and just living through a Stage One experience can be a very stressful and difficult experience. But one thing is very clear. It is not until we have met and overcome all the challenges and obstacles of Stage One that we will be ready to embrace the challenges of Stage Two. Our next step on the path.

The Fool has now taken the first step of his journey and is about to unknowingly step off a cliff to plunge into the unknown. The Hero or Heroine is still at home enjoying the experience of a normal life, totally unaware of the upheaval ahead. The Soul, grounded in the security and comfort of the root chakra is sensing that something, somehow, is energetically shifting.

Summary of Stage One of the Soul's Path/ Characteristics of a Stage One soul

* The soul is unaware that they are on a soul journey.
* The soul is predominantly driven by ego and self-preservation.
* Stage One souls consider themselves to be 'normal people' (whatever the definition).
* They follow a 'normal lifestyle'.
* Can be very intelligent, well-educated and highly respected.
* Can also be people suffering with issues, homeless, poor.
* Have developed their own belief system, philosophy, ethos, moral code.
* Tendency to be overly concerned about money.
* Materialistic/Consumerist and like acquiring 'things'.
* Competitive at work, sport, socially.
* Career-focused.
* Read novels, watch mainstream TV.
* Use social media, facebook, Twitter.
* Need peer-acceptance.
* Not good listeners/very opinionated.
* Narrow-minded.
* Can be aggressive if challenged.

* Scientific, rational, sceptical, cynical.
* Put their trust in the five senses.
* 'Prove it to me' mentality.
* Total focus is on themselves and their own wellbeing.
* Sceptical of spirituality and spiritual people.
* Don't like their philosophy of life challenged.

STAGE TWO

*"A single event can awaken within us
a stranger totally unknown to us".*
Antoine de Saint-Exupery

CHAKRA: TWO (WATER)

Sanskrit Name - 'Svadhisthana'
Location - Lower abdomen/sexual organs
Colour - Orange
Common Name - 'Sacral' chakra
Characteristics - The focus is on flexibility rather than rigidity. There is more fluidity, movement, a willingness to change, more openness, less self-gratification, more focus on personal relationships, a move from 'masculine' to 'feminine' energy, a move from 'closed mind' to 'receptive mind'.

Tarot Card: "The Fool'

The Fool is now at the start of his journey. He carries all his hopes and dreams in a small bag attached to a stick he carries on his shoulder. In traditional Tarot card imagery he (or she) is about to step unawares over a cliff edge. The Fool represents new beginnings and untapped potential and reflects someone about to step forward with both innocence, ignorance and trust into the unknown. Life is about to change forever but the future is uncertain and the destination is still a mystery.

Hero's Journey: 'The Call to Adventure'

The Hero receives an unexpected 'Call to Adventure'. Something has changed and it has caused a disruption to normality. Routine has suddenly been disturbed by a new event that heralds a need for change to happen. The 'familiar' is now under threat and the Hero is required to break out of old habit patterns and thoughts in order to face up to a new challenge. This requires leaving the 'old' world behind and having the courage to set off on a new journey to an unknown destination.

How do we recognise a 'Stage Two' soul and what makes them different from a 'Stage One' soul? On the face of it the differences are very slight and very marginal; it is actually very difficult to spot the differences.

Just like the Stage One soul, a Stage Two soul mostly enjoys all the same things and shares the same life philosophy. Both probably go to work to earn a living, save for a mortgage and a car, raise a family, enjoy foreign holidays and watch TV. They probably own mobile phones, use Social Media, go out with friends, enjoy a beer or glass of wine and try to do the best they can in a tough 'dog-eat-dog' world where you have to fight to earn respect and keep a roof over your head. For that's the reality of life.

The transition from Stage One of our soul path into Stage Two is as 'blurred' as every other stage transition. It is not a sudden event but a gradual, subtle and gentle passage from one way of 'being' to another. But there is something rather special and different about Stage Two that is uncommon during the other stages and usually unique to the 'Stage One - Stage Two' borderline. This is because something happens to us when we are in Stage One that eventually propels us - usually unknowingly - into Stage Two. This 'thing' that happens to us is different for every individual but has a common origin. In spiritual texts the borderline between the world we perceive as reality and the spirit world is likened to a thin veil that separates the two realities. And the something that happens to us whilst we are happily ensconced into the comfort of our Stage One existence can best be described as a *"parting of the veil."*

It is, more often than not, an unanticipated event that gives us a glimpse of the spiritual reality that has always been running in parallel with our Earth Plane reality, even though we have previously chosen to ignore it. It always arrives as an unexpected intrusion into our normal life which forces us to start thinking differently about everything we thought we knew. It is the catalyst that knocks us sideways out of our comfort zone and into a new unknown territory.

So, what exactly is this catalyst that shakes us up and forces us to think differently?

There is no definitive answer to this question because the catalyst is always a very individual experience but there are many good examples. And interestingly, if these examples have one common theme it is this - the down-to-earth, rationalist, sceptical, scientific, practical Stage One soul suddenly comes head-on and face-to-face with something that cannot be rationally explained within their perceived world-view. And now the rationalist is left scratching his or her head in bewilderment. It is as if the friend I mentioned earlier really did find a UFO had landed in his back garden!

The catalyst could be something like the sudden death of a close friend or family member that raises questions about mortality, death, the 'point' of life or even the afterlife or heaven and hell. But it is not always related to death.

Sometimes it is an incredible synchronicity. Something far more profound than a mere co-incidence and something that is difficult to rationally explain. It might be a million-to-one synchronicity that is completely inexplicable, or it might be a very close personal encounter with death involving a 'Near Death Experience' or 'NDE'.

In other instances, it might involve a dream, a vision or a revelation. It may even be a message from the spirit world via a psychic or medium who reveals a truth only known to the recipient. It could be a physical encounter with someone who is deeply spiritual or the first-hand experience of an unexplained phenomena that seems to break the rules of physics. It might be a UFO encounter or ghost encounter or another paranormal experience. It might be a nature spirit or fairy encounter. In some cases, it could even just be a beautiful moment in deep woodland or beside the sea where a sudden sense of one's true nature in the bigger scheme of things is revealed - a sudden revelation or deep insight that seems to come out of thin air.

Or it could be none of these things.

It might be as simple as waking up one morning with nothing other than a 'peculiar feeling' that has a spiritual twist. Something that must never be disclosed at work, at home or with family or fellow sceptics - but rather something that has to remain private and filed away in the brain simply labelled as 'unexplained'.

Whatever the catalyst might be, Stage Two always starts with some kind of an awakening or calling. Something totally unexpected has happened that changes everything about how we used to view the world. Our normal worldview has been rocked by something that defies rational explanation and at first it feels very uncomfortable. But now a seed has been sown and the feeling won't go away.

When this happens the Stage One soul suddenly finds himself or herself in a new, and slightly uncomfortable, state of mind. They are suddenly in uncharted territory. He or she still desperately wants to cling to the safe rationalities of the Stage One life experience but is now struggling. Life is not quite what it is supposed to be - because something 'weird' has happened that doesn't fit in with how things are supposed to be. This situation requires making a very tough and very difficult choice - to completely ignore this unexplained anomaly and simply to assign it to the 'ignore and forget it' bin. Or to accept it and embrace it.

Slowly, over time, the newly arrived Stage Two soul starts to assimilate this weird experience into their world view and now starts to take a mild interest in other weird things because something has shocked them out of their previous complacency and caused them to question one of their previous realities or certainties.

Now, the newly arrived Stage Two soul is seeking an answer. Seeking a truth. Something they previously believed in has proved to be flawed and now they need to know why. This is also slightly scary for them because their status quo has been compromised and they are out of their depth - but suddenly very fascinated.

This new fascination, stimulated by the awakening or revelation, causes a shift in their interests and suddenly things that a Stage One soul might find of little or no interest become much more interesting to a newly awakened Stage Two soul who now starts to read about other strange or unexplained things like amazing coincidences or weird news. These new interests have been engendered by a disturbance in their traditional perception of what constitutes normality. These anomalies therefore need to be investigated - if only to disprove them - so that normality can be restored and life can get back to where it was before the disturbance rudely shook things up.

But getting back to the comforts and certainties of a Stage One existence is not easily achieved. And, try as they might, the newly evolved Stage Two soul soon realises - and eventually has to accept - that life will never be quite the same again. Something out of the ordinary has unbalanced their view of what constitutes reality and grabbed their attention and slightly shifted their thinking. And now they just can't seem to get rid of this annoying and irrational revelation.

But this 'new knowledge' brings with it, other secondary feelings which are still, at this stage of the soul's development, mostly ego-driven. This is because new Stage Two souls might feel that this awakening has given them new insights into life which they didn't have before. So, in a way, they are now more enlightened than they used to be. In their mind - and in particular in their subconscious - this gives them a sense of advantage over their friends and colleagues who have yet to acquire this new knowledge and therefore entitles them to be slightly condescending to those who are less well informed! But, paradoxically and equally, it also makes them slightly less prejudiced towards those strange and weird people who believe in all this type of nonsense.

Gradually, over time, the Stage Two soul starts to gain more confidence about their newly enhanced world view. And, as the weird experience becomes more deeply assimilated into their overall philosophy about life, a sort of smugness sets in. The previous rational-sceptic has now discovered a new truth about the way the world works which makes him or her now feel very superior to those clueless Stage One-ers!

But one thing has not changed despite the Stage One soul morphing into a Stage Two soul. And that is the ego. The constantly chattering ego - the 'monkey mind' - still rules the roost and despite a shift in awareness about the probable existence of some sort of spiritual dimension to reality, the overall approach to life in general remains much the same. The washing still needs to be done, the bills still need to be paid and the children still need taking to school. Something has undoubtedly shifted but, for the newly advanced Stage Two soul, thankfully, most things have stayed much the same.

To understand the key differences between a Stage One and Stage Two soul is to recognise that for the Stage Two soul the world has now been changed forever. Something has inexplicably appeared in their lives that has challenged them to take a new look at things that were previously accepted as completely normal. Something unusual and out-of-the-ordinary has forced them out of their 'comfortably numb' trance and shifted their awareness. Most of their friends, family and acquaintances are still mostly Stage One souls - cynical but reliable - but now there is a new-found tolerance of other souls that have had similar revelations. The Stage One soul is now ready and open to nervously applying for membership of the 'Stage Two Club'.

Now there can be no going back. The twists and turns of the soul's path have brought them this far and now the mysteries of the path ahead are beckoning for those brave enough to take the next step.

The Fool has now stepped off the cliff and plunged into the unknown with innocence and courage not knowing where he or she is going to land. The Hero or Heroine has had their life suddenly disturbed by an external event which has challenged their belief system and propelled them into movement. The Soul, previously grounded in the security and comfort of the root chakra, has now felt an energy shift that has moved its awareness up the spine to the sacral chakra which feels more open to change.

Summary of Stage Two of the Soul's Path/ Characteristics of a Stage Two soul

* Basically, the same as a Level One soul in many respects.
* But something has 'happened' to them.
* There has been a 'catalyst': the death of someone close or an inexplicable synchronicity.
* They have met someone extraordinary or had a ghost or UFO encounter.
* There has been a dream-vision or premonition, an NDE or paranormal experience.
* Something that can't be rationally explained has shaken their world view.
* Their 'comfort zone' has been challenged.
* They want 'normality' back - but they know intuitively that life can never be quite the same again.
* There has been a 'Parting of the Veil' - an 'Awakening'.
* There is a growing realisation that there is more to life than they thought.
* They are more open to exploring this new opportunity to evolve.
* The cynic is now more open to persuasion.

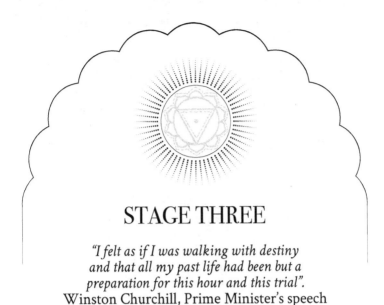

STAGE THREE

*"I felt as if I was walking with destiny
and that all my past life had been but a
preparation for this hour and this trial".*
Winston Churchill, Prime Minister's speech

CHAKRA: THREE (FIRE)

Sanskrit Name - 'Manipura'
Location - Below the sternum - over the stomach
Colour - Yellow
Common Name - 'Solar Plexus' chakra
Characteristics - The focus is on seeking truth and
wisdom and a search for purpose. The element of
'fire' has generated more energy and awakened a
heightened consciousness - the starting point for
transformation, self-esteem, confidence, power
and freedom of choice.

Tarot Card: 'The Magician'

*The Magician represents our 'Guardian Angel' because
in Tarot tradition the Magician is the guide that helps
and supports us on our soul journey. The Fool has
started out on his journey in innocence and ignorance
with no sense of where he is going. But now he has met
the Magician who is the guide to the spiritual realms.
Magicians are the manipulators of unseen forces*

and energies and their display of magic reveals the potential of exploring new possibilities and opening new doorways into other realities. In some Tarot pack imagery the Magician stands at a fork in the road signifying choice. The choices are clear - return back to where you started (the road back to normality and ignorance) or take the road into the unknown (the road to your destiny and enlightenment).

Hero's Journey: 'The Crossing of the First Threshold'

The Hero, at first reluctant to leave the safety of home behind, has now accepted the 'Call to Adventure' and has set off on the journey into the unknown. But the Hero has now arrived at the border between the reality he or she has always known and a new reality that is unfamiliar and a little frightening. The Hero is thus standing at the threshold of the unknown, nervous and uncertain. But a new feeling has suddenly entered the Hero's mind. Some form of inexplicable 'supernatural aid' has appeared to reassure the Hero that it is safe to move forward without fear.

⚜

If we were to term a 'Stage One' soul as a 'Materialist' for argument's sake (not a perfect term but useful as a temporary label) and a 'Stage Two' soul as a 'Materialist with a slight interest in the spiritual' then we could also describe a Stage Two soul as someone with a foot in both camps. And that is probably a good way of thinking about all those people we meet on our journey through life who are living within the first two stages of their soul journey. It simply helps us to remember the distinction. These descriptions might not be perfect, but they are useful in terms of providing a temporary 'anchor point' to help us recognise where our friends and loved ones are on their own unique and personal soul journeys.

When a soul arrives at 'Stage Two' of their soul journey it can still take many years before they are ready to progress to the third level of soul maturity at Stage Three. And this is exactly how it should be. Souls are never rushed through any of the stages because the whole soul experience requires many lifetimes to flourish and mature. It is true to say that we all progress at different rates according to our uniqueness and our personality and - to a degree - our tenacity in facing up to life's challenges. Quite simply, this is the universal law we all have to abide by.

Some of us will have experienced hundreds of previous lives and some of us will have experienced thousands of previous lives. But it is not the *number* of previous lives we have experienced that determines our progress on the soul path. It is all about whether or not we have learned the lessons we needed to learn and whether we have overcome the challenges and obstacles that have been our testing ground on that journey. Sometimes we have to lead many different lives time and time again because we have still not 'passed the test'. We have been faced with the same, or very similar, challenges but have still not worked out how to overcome them. Only when we have faced up to these challenges and taken the right action to obtain the right outcome do we start to progress to the next level.

So, let's now take a look at those souls who have successfully faced the challenges of Stage One and Stage Two and overcome them - and now stand at the threshold of their next soul journey challenge - Stage Three.

We have already seen how a soul in Stage One is primarily focused on what they perceive to be the real world because it can be seen and touched. For ego-driven Stage One souls the real world is a tough, competitive, difficult, frustrating and often violent place where you have to fight to survive. Anything that falls outside of this mode of thinking - or is not material enough because it can't be touched, smelled, heard, tasted or seen is mentally and emotionally discarded as being untrue or wishy-washy airy-fairy nonsense. Remember that the favourite phrase of a typical Level One soul is "Prove it!". Stage One souls love to see hard proof and unequivocal evidence so it is unwise to engage a Level One soul in a conversation about unicorns or mermaids, fairies or aliens! Do so at your peril!

By the time a Level One soul has matured into a Level Two soul they are more open-minded about such unscientific and unproven things. Now, at least, and at last, they will probably listen and may even express a more balanced view. They may also talk more openly about spiritual things to a degree - even if with slight embarrassment. This is because Level Two souls still share the same broad down-to-earth life philosophy as a Level One soul, but they are now awakened souls. They have had an experience of something out-of-the-ordinary that they couldn't explain, and it has now whetted their appetite to learn more about this strange unseen world that we call the 'spiritual'.

A Level Three soul is therefore very similar to a Level Two soul, but the main difference is their greater acceptance of the spiritual dimension of existence. Whereas a Level Two soul will have an *interest* in spiritual matters (unlike a Level One soul) a Level Three soul will now be starting to actively seek more information and answers about the spiritual realms. If a Level Two soul is still confused by their spiritual awakening and not yet sure how to deal with it – then a Level Three soul is determined to look deeper and find answers (The Level One soul, of course, is completely *uninterested* because the idea of any sort of a spirit world is complete poppycock!).

So in short, a Level Three soul is now on a quest to find answers to questions like: 'What is this spiritual stuff all about?', 'Is there really life after death?', 'Are souls really immortal?', 'What exactly is the real meaning of life?', 'Why am I here?' and 'What is my life purpose?' etcetera. It was the American author, Mark Twain, who once said, *"The two most important days in your life are the day you are born and the day you found out why"* and this is the perfect description for a third level soul who has been recently awakened to realise that he or she is here for a very definite purpose.

The hesitancy and slight scepticism of the Level Two soul has now disappeared, and the newly enlightened Third Level soul is on a determined mission to find real answers. They feel less embarrassed about the stigma of being interested in alternative views of reality and they are now on a quest to find out more.

This can be a daunting and often frightening quest for a new Level Three soul. The certainties and stability they enjoyed during levels one and two are now fading fast and this new reality they have now discovered is not yet grounded in anything substantial that can be clung on to with any certainty. A soul embarking into this third level of existence is like a sailor on a rudderless ship on an unknown ocean. They have no map or compass to guide their way. Some of their friends and colleagues will notice this new aspect of the Level Three's personality and may think they are acting strangely or are getting confused. The reality of course, is that the Level Three soul has now accepted that they are on some kind of mission to find the truth about something elusive and non-material, but still don't know exactly what it is they are looking for.

Where does the journey end? Is there some kind of pot of treasure? What lies at the end of the rainbow? Setting off on a mission with no goal in sight seems a foolish thing to do and takes a lot of courage. The overriding question for all Level Three souls at this stage, is how do you cope when most of your friends and family are still at Stage One or Stage Two? How can you possibly explain to them what's going through your mind or what you are seeking?

A good analogy for this stage of development, as we have already seen, is the first card of the Tarot - "The Fool". The Fool is usually depicted as an innocent young man blissfully unaware that he is stepping off a cliff edge into the unknown. He does this with little idea where he is going but feels compelled to find his way in the world and to seek truth and wisdom. This is the perfect metaphor for a newly established Stage Three Soul who, having left the challenges of Stage Two behind, is now ready to face new insights, challenges and adventures on the soul path ahead. They now feel prepared and courageous enough to take that metaphorical step off the cliff and face up to whatever might happen.

In terms of our relationships with friends, family and loved ones this transition from Stage Two to Stage Three can be a momentous challenge. All over the world are couples who fell in love when they were both at Stage One sharing the same views, goals, aspirations and dreams and looking forward to a lifelong partnership on their journey together. Then, sometimes many years later 'he' is still at Stage One, but 'she' has now progressed to Stage Three and a communication breakdown has now ensued. It is as though they are no longer speaking the same language and their views on 'life' and 'spirituality' are at complete odds with each other. He simply cannot understand why his wife has become so 'difficult' or why she has got so involved with airy-fairy and new-age things. She cannot understand why her husband remains so closed-minded and won't accept that there are things out there in the universe beyond his understanding.

Try as they might to bridge the gap or find some kind of compromise the relationship is essentially doomed to failure unless they can find an acceptable middle ground. And while it is true to say that sometimes even a Level One soul and a Level Seven soul can enjoy a good relationship, it is actually extremely rare.

So, what else characterises a Level Three soul besides their quest to learn more about spiritual matters? There are a few other traits that are common to Third Level souls that are worth examining.

Along with a more open-minded attitude in general and a willingness to learn more about the unseen world of spirit, a Third Level soul will also demonstrate a greater thirst for knowledge. Instead of being satisfied by what they learned at school, college or university - and what skills they acquired in their career - they are now on a new quest to learn about a much wider range of subjects. They will be drawn to read books and watch documentaries on much more esoteric subjects like UFO's, Conspiracy Theories, Reincarnation, Religion, Philosophy, Alternative Health, Meditation, Yoga or Spiritual practices. Their eyes and their minds have been widened and they now have a much greater interest in things that, not so long ago, were of little importance or interest to them. They have discovered a new thirst for knowledge and are willing to expand their horizons.

Friends who are still at Level One or Two are now viewed with caution because they are now perceived as being unenlightened and even boring. The quest for new knowledge is now insatiable and has become a key driving force in their life. They now take a much greater interest in philosophical ideas about things like truth and justice and watch the daily News with a greater sense of empathy for those who are suffering because of global conflict or injustice. They also have more interest in alternative sources of information which popularise new ideas including new politics or new economics etc. They have become more interested in global matters rather than just parochial news and are becoming better informed about world events.

For some Level Three souls who have enjoyed a number of incarnations at the Level Three stage there may be another aspect that has started to emerge slowly and almost imperceptibly. It starts as a vague feeling that, if given enough attention, might develop into something interesting. It is a sense that they are being accompanied on their journey by some unseen and fleeting presence, not substantial enough to be labelled or identified yet, but sometimes sensed more strongly when occasionally hovering somewhere just on the edge of vision. Another mystery to be attended to in due course.

This, of course, is their eternal guide - their Guardian Angel. Ever present, but always too elusive to contact directly due to the interference of the ego who is determined to get in the way. One of the ego's highest priorities is to stop the soul connecting to its Guardian Angel because, if that happens, the ego immediately loses its power.

Level Three souls are still predominantly materialistic and still biased in some of their thinking because, let's face it, they still have a home to maintain or a business to run. But this 'spiritual thing' is now much too fascinating to be ignored and it has started to open all sorts of new doors into other equally fascinating subjects.

Pandora's box has now been thrown wide open and who knows what it might reveal?

The Fool has now found himself before a Magician who is actually a Spirit Guide who is able to introduce the Fool to the mysteries of the spirit world. The Fool is fascinated and feels ready to listen to what the Magician has to say. The Hero or Heroine is now standing at the threshold of the unknown, nervous and uncertain. But now some form of inexplicable supernatural aid has appeared to reassure the Hero that it is safe to move forward without fear and the Hero now feels ready to face up to whatever challenges might lie ahead. The Soul has now felt another energy shift that has moved its awareness further up the spine to a point just below the rib cage. There is a sense of an awakened consciousness that is anticipating some form of transformation and a sense of excitement is building.

Summary of Stage Three of the Soul's Path/ Characteristics of a Stage Three soul

❋ More open to new ideas and new philosophies of life.

❋ Reading less novels and starting to read more about unusual or odd things.

❋ Seeking out interesting TV documentaries or films on wider subjects.

❋ Still predominantly ego-driven but opening up to more radical ideas.

❋ Starting to ask the big questions.

❋ More willing to listen and learn with an open mind.

❋ Confidence about knowing everything has been dented, so now more open.

❋ On a mission to find real answers because "This spirituality thing needs to be understood...".

❋ Increasing interest in asking "What if...?" re past lives, spirit world, karma etc.

❋ A sense of 'another' being hovering around from time to time.

❋ Stage Three starts with an open mind and usually ends with a certainty.

STAGE FOUR

"I'm just a soul whose intentions are good,
Oh Lord, please don't let me be misunderstood".
Nina Simone

CHAKRA: FOUR (LOVE)

Sanskrit Name - 'Anahata'
Location - Middle of the chest
Colour - Green
Common Name - 'Heart' chakra
Characteristics - The focus is on moving from body consciousness to spirit consciousness and a recognition of the need to lose the ego. A need for more integration of love, peace, forgiveness and compassion in life plus an awareness of one's 'state of being' from all perspectives including the need to let go of old modes of thinking and old habits.

Tarot Card: 'The High Priestess'

The Fool's journey has now led him to meet 'The High Priestess' which in Tarot imagery is represented by an ethereal spiritual woman who stands at the foot of a stairway between two pillars, one black and one white. In her hand she holds a pomegranate. The black pillar represents the darkness of ignorance and the white pillar purity and enlightenment. The stairway represents the soul's steady ascension on the spiritual path and the pomegranate represents the seeds of an as-yet undeveloped potential. The High Priestess represents the 'inner world' and the powers of intuition. The Fool now has to make a very difficult choice. To embrace his or her inner calling that is opening up the realities of the spiritual realms - or to remain in the comfort zone of ignorance.

Hero's Journey: 'The Road of Trials'

The Hero has found the courage - aided by the supernatural realms - to cross the threshold and face whatever challenges lie ahead without fear. Now the trials, obstacles and challenges are coming thick and fast. The certainties and familiarities of the Hero's former world are now crumbling as new realities open up that challenge his or her deepest convictions and belief systems. Self-doubt and uncertainty are replacing the old feelings of superiority and ego-driven decision making - but the 'quest' has begun and now there is no going back.

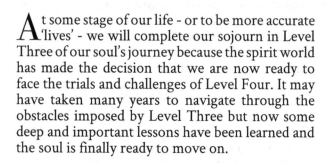

At some stage of our life - or to be more accurate 'lives' - we will complete our sojourn in Level Three of our soul's journey because the spirit world has made the decision that we are now ready to face the trials and challenges of Level Four. It may have taken many years to navigate through the obstacles imposed by Level Three but now some deep and important lessons have been learned and the soul is finally ready to move on.

There may well be a feeling of great achievement when this happens because our soul is now seemingly making significant progress from the ego-centric, sceptical disbeliever of Stage One, through the spiritual awakening of Stage Two and the new exciting discoveries made in Stage Three.

Surely then, this is a cause for celebration?

Well, unfortunately it's not actually quite so simple or straightforward as that. Stage Four is probably one of the most difficult stages to get through - and for very good reason.

It always starts with a crisis. A crisis that many call the 'Dark night of the Soul'.

This might at first seem a paradox. Why would the spirit world be so mean as to reward you with a crisis just as you are beginning to make great spiritual progress on your path? It doesn't seem fair!

The reality is neither fair or unfair it just 'is' - and that fact can be quite hard to swallow when you are already struggling to move forward on your soul's journey.

Let's examine why this crisis always happens at the start of Stage Four and let's try to make sense of it.

As a Stage Three soul your fascination with the spiritual dimension of life has been awakened and you have been super-curious to learn more. You have been reading loads of books and trying to fathom how this whole 'spiritual thing' works and hangs together. You may well have attended a few talks or watched a few films that have been gradually increasing your awareness. You may even have spoken to a few close friends about what you have discovered and those at Level One or Two have probably frowned and affected disinterest while those at Levels Five and Six have nodded sagely and smiled at you as if to say, "of course! Welcome to the real reality".

You now feel more comfortable and knowledgeable about subjects that previously were of little interest to you and there have been many times when you felt like a child excited about being given a new toy. Sure, you can still deal perfectly adequately with all the day-to-day pressures of work, home and family and you still enjoy watching your favourite TV programmes or going out for a drink with friends - but now you have a new interest in your life. You have become immensely fascinated by esoteric subjects and you have started to grasp how things like karma and reincarnation fit into your mental model of how the universe works. And the fascination of it all has grabbed your attention like never before and it won't let go.

But one day, when you least expect it, something significant happens that will propel you out of the comfort of your Level Three life into the scary reality of Level Four. It always comes in a sudden flash - just like a flash of 'inspiration' but in this case it isn't inspiration. It is more like a flash of realisation or revelation. It might happen while you are peacefully reading a book or mowing the lawn. Or it might happen when you are driving to work or working out at the gym. This Level Four sudden flash of insight can come at any time and in any place. And usually it comes at you in such an out of the blue fashion that you might be left completely speechless and in shock for some time afterwards. It is a metaphorical sudden slap in the face. A wake-up call you were not expecting!

When this happens, this sudden and unexpected 'flash of realisation' will rock you to your core. It will send shivers down your spine and cause sweat to break out on your brow and it will knock the foundations of your life from right under your feet.

This insight will suddenly plunge your whole life into crisis because the truth of the insight is unquestionable. There is no room for doubt or conjecture. No room for debate. The spirit world has delivered a message to you like a telegram from the stars and you know with every fibre of your being that the message is true.

So, what is this message? This insight? This revelation? This realisation that plunges a Level Four soul into such a state of crisis?

In the simplest of terms, it is this: The Level Four soul suddenly realises without a shadow of a doubt that everything he or she has always thought about the world they live in is *wrong*. Reality has been turned on its head and all the certainties about how the world operates have been shattered in an instant.

Up until now, as a Level Three soul, reading about spiritual things has been an academic exercise. A fascination. Like reading a book about Astronomy or Archaeology or Flower Arranging. Just reading to gather information intellectually. Yes, we can all read about UFO's or ghosts or leprechauns, but it doesn't mean we have to *believe* any of it. It's just *interesting*.

The Level Three soul has opened the door into a new world. A new way of thinking. And now the Level Four soul has 'picked up the baton' and continued this enjoyable intellectual exercise. He or she has read about the spiritual realms, about energy healing, about past lives and reincarnation, about chakras and auras the laws of karma and soul contracts and Source and it has been a hugely enjoyable and eye-opening exercise. But it has just been a reading exercise. Following the words on a page.

But in that revelatory moment - when the flash of insight comes through like a bolt of lightning into your head - it changes *everything*. Because now you are no longer reading an interesting book or watching an interesting movie.

You are now the *subject* of the book. You are now *in* the movie! You are living it for real!

And this time, and for the first time in your life, you know for certain that the spiritual realms are unquestionably *real* and that the material world you have been living in all your life is *false* - it is all just an illusion.

Why is this a crisis? Because yesterday, as a newly arrived Level Four, you were very comfortable with life generally, but today everything has changed and been turned on its head. Not just changed for today, but for evermore. So, the Level Four soul desperately tries to rationalise what has just happened...

"Life hasn't always been perfect, but at least it made sense. I'm just a physical flesh and blood person. We are born - we live our life - we die. We work to earn a living. We fall in love, we get married, we have children and do the best we can with what we've got. The world is 'real' because we can physically touch things like a car or a house or a tree. Day follows night and the sky is blue and the sun is always yellow. Books about spirituality are just 'books'. Nobody actually knows if they are factual. Everything is just as it should be...or at least I thought it was...".

Today all those certainties have been thrown into total disarray and the Level Four soul's mind starts racing and trying to assimilate this new revelation:

"Wait a minute. That's all wrong! I'm not really just flesh and blood. I'm just composed of millions of vibrations. I'm really an immortal soul just here on Earth for a brief time to learn important stuff. I've had hundreds or thousands of past lives and I keep being reincarnated. I even have a guardian angel watching over me - but how do I make contact? I'm here for some kind of purpose or mission. I agreed to some kind of 'Soul Contract' with my Spirit Guides last time I was between lives. Oh my God! What did I promise to do? I've forgotten! What am I supposed to do now? How can I explain all this to my kids? How am I going to cope at work tomorrow? What will my friends think of me? Everyone will think I've gone crazy...".

It is probably true to say that this Level Four crisis is without doubt one of the most difficult moments of our life and one we may have had to endure many times over many lifetimes. Everything we knew for certain has been 'thrown out the window' and we cannot reclaim it. For once we know this truth there can be no going back. We cannot retreat into the safety cocoon of being a Level Three soul again. We are now stuck with the stark truth. And now we somehow have to learn to deal with it.

For those who have always followed a particular religion during this incarnation and followed the teachings of holy books or holy leaders and adopted a faith, this flash of insight can be particularly life-changing and shocking. If their faith is related to religious beliefs that support the afterlife then this confirmation of the soul's eternity can be of great comfort. But for those whose faith does *not* accept the concept of an afterlife the spirit world revelation can be discomforting and very challenging to deal with.

Once we do come to terms with what we have learned in this moment of revelation however, then life slowly gets back on track. Our sense of what constitutes normality has been changed forever - so we now have to start learning how to live in a new mode of reality that will bring fresh challenges in its own way. Gradually, slowly and over time, we learn to embrace this new mode of thinking spiritually until it becomes our new norm. And, eventually, we start to feel comfortable with it. And then, thankfully, we actually start to enjoy it.

We now know the answer to one of life's greatest questions - "Why we are here?" and we now realise and fully accept that we are all on a mission to complete our soul contract. That, in a nutshell, *is* the purpose of life.

The crisis is now over. But new challenges have just begun and now we need new tools and strategies to deal with them. Our old tools that helped us to navigate our world through Stages One to Three are now redundant and some need to be permanently discarded. New ways of dealing with everything from a totally new perspective are called for.

After the crisis has settled and peace has been restored, the Level Four soul now has to face the challenges ahead - but this time with a new set of tools and a new deep understanding of how the spirit world really works. But the Level Four soul is still here on the Earth Plane with all the normal day-to-day challenges to deal with that we all have to face.

At Levels One to Three the main pre-occupation was dealing with the daily trials and tribulations of human existence. A career to follow, a family to feed, bills to pay, chores to be done etcetera. All those challenges still remain to be dealt with, but now there is an added dimension that also needs to be factored in - the need to simultaneously follow a path that enables the tasks agreed in the soul contract to be tackled and completed too. And for some souls this means that the task list has now been doubled.

The insight or revelation that the Level Four soul has received always leads to a number of significant changes in the soul's life at this point in time. It is because of their new-found awareness of their true nature as an immortal soul - rather than just a physical body that will one day simply 'die'.

Just having this awareness tends to change the way everything in life is now viewed and there are many shifts of personality and attitude that accompany this shift. Let's look at some typical examples.

A Level Four soul will still have a lot of internal conflicts following the moment of insight - and for many years this internal conflict will continuously rage within them. But, gradually, over time such feelings will dissipate and dissolve away.

They will spend an increasing amount of time on personal introspection and take themselves into a semi-meditative state to think things through much more deeply than before. They will be very interested in real world affairs - politics, wars, social injustices, climate change, revolutions etcetera but will spend more time on researching the real truth behind the flimsy façade of the mainstream media news on TV and in newspapers. Their compassion for the 'underdog' will be more pronounced, their sense of what true justice constitutes will be more sharpened and their moral and ethical 'compass' will be in overdrive.

Up until this point their life will have been fairly straightforward, ordered and structured (subject of course to their individual Soul Contract challenges) but now the future is uncertain because a new mode of thinking about the world has been introduced. Level Four souls now start asking themselves questions like, 'What is my place in the world?' or 'How does immortality change my understanding of what life and death really mean?'. They will also start to think more deeply about Earth Plane relationships and their dynamics as well as the implications of relationships in the spirit world. They will think about their current partner and try to see how this revelation is going to affect their relationship moving forward. They will reflect on where they are in life at this point in time and depending on whether they are still young, middle-aged or elderly, will reflect on the years ahead.

To a degree, the revelation has introduced some frustration and uncertainty. Not everything works as was first thought and everything in life is more complex now. The new insights are proving challenging and old paradigms and previously held world-views need to shift. Some fundamentally held beliefs are now changing and a wider perspective is called for in order to face up to both real-world challenges and spiritual-world challenges. How is this going to be achieved and what are partners, children, relatives, work colleagues, friends and neighbours going to think?

And how much of what other people think really matters anymore?

The Level Four soul's mind is now full of perpetual questions that are causing him or her some distress:

"How am I going to follow this spiritual path? How do I achieve everything I agreed to in my Soul Contract? How can I deal with everything in my normal life while all this is going on? And how do I explain all this to my partner who is already telling me I am acting strangely lately?"

Souls who have arrived at Level Four often have to stay at this level for many years because the implications of their awakening are so profound. The 'Dark Night of the Soul' has been a long tough journey. But now, at last, there seems to be light at the end of the tunnel.

It is the light that is drawing them inexorably towards 'Level Five' of their soul path.

The Fool has learned to trust the spiritual guidance of The Magician who has now led him or her to meet The High Priestess - the personification of spiritual wisdom. The Fool has now had to make a very difficult choice - to embrace his or her 'inner calling' that is opening up the realities of the spiritual realms - or to remain in the comfort zone of ignorance. The Fool has chosen to follow the road to enlightenment. The Hero or Heroine's former conceptions of reality have now crumbled away as new realities have opened up that have challenged his or her deepest convictions and belief systems. Now there is no going back. The 'Road of Trials' lies ahead and must be faced with courage. The Soul is now operating at the 'Heart Chakra' level and has moved from body consciousness to spirit consciousness. Now is the time to lose the ego by refocusing on love, peace, forgiveness and compassion and also the time to let go of old habits and old ways of thinking.

Summary of Stage Four of the Soul's Path/ Characteristics of a Stage Four soul

* A plunge into crisis - the 'dark night of the soul', confusion, fear, uncertainty.
* The sceptical soul has now been fully awakened to new truths.
* Full acceptance of the spiritual realms and truth of the soul's existence.
* Full acceptance of past lives, immortality, healing energy, spirit guides.
* Full acceptance of being on a spiritual journey and path.
* Interested in getting in touch with their spiritual guides.
* Shock - 'Everything I thought I 'knew' is wrong! I have to accept this new reality'.
* Possible relationship issues.
* New interests/more open/fascinated/enquiring.
* Facing up to the big questions: 'How do I now live my life as an immortal soul?'
* How do I find out what I agreed to in my 'Soul Contract?'
* How is my life going to change in the future?
* What do I do next?

STAGE FIVE

*"If you do not change direction
you may end up where you are heading".*
Lao Tzu (6th Century BC)

CHAKRA: FIVE (SOUND)

Sanskrit Name - 'Visuddha'
Location - Neck
Colour - Blue
Common Name - 'Throat' chakra
Characteristics - The focus is on honest and open communication, speaking and language, connection to others, self-knowledge, creativity, spiritual growth, higher vibration thinking, synthesising new concepts and ideas, personal integrity, honesty and healing.

Tarot Card: 'The Hierophant'

The Fool has learned a great deal from his meetings with The Magician and The High Priestess and with renewed vigour has followed the soul path that has now brought him to the Hierophant. In Tarot imagery, The Hierophant is portrayed as a mythical Centaur with the body of a horse and the upper torso of a man. In one of his hands he holds a scroll. The Hierophant is a 'wisdom keeper' or 'spiritual teacher' and the scroll contains the written wisdom of the divine. The Fool has now made the firm decision to follow his or her spiritual path and now seeks wisdom and truth. When The Fool meets The Hierophant he is taught about the true nature of the immortal soul and the true purpose of his or her journey.

Hero's Journey: 'The Meeting with the Goddess'

The Hero has now faced all the challenges and trials and finally overcome them. The 'dragon' of 'ignorance and ego' has now been slain and the Hero has emerged victorious. The Hero was not expecting any particular reward for overcoming the spectres and mistakes from his or her own past but a reward is waiting. A 'Goddess' has now appeared before the Hero following the success of overcoming the final challenge. She is the symbol of wisdom and holds within her the keys to enlightenment. She stands ready to be the Hero's guide on the next part of the journey.

———※———

There are a number of significant differences between a soul at Level Four on their spiritual path and those at Level Five but also a number of very marginal differences where distinctions are blurred.

Perhaps the biggest distinction between the two levels, however, is in terms of how a Level Four soul and a Level Five soul deals with this new revelation that the spiritual world is not just an abstract concept, but a very real phenomenon.

If, for example's sake, 'Susan' is a Level Four soul and overhears two friends talking about her, the friends might say something like:

"I don't know what is happening to Susan. She's gone all spiritual and weird lately..."

A Level Four soul would probably be very upset and possibly offended by this remark and may even want to prove to her friends that this is not the case and that she is still the same 'Susan' they have always known. It's just that she now has an interest in more spiritual things.

This is because all Level Four souls are still predominantly driven by their ego and in this example their ego has been attacked and it must therefore be defended at all costs.

If, however, Susan is now a Level Five soul, then her friends' words will simply bounce off her like raindrops off an umbrella or arrows off a shield. Susan will not be upset or offended in the slightest because she has now learned to subdue the ego and actually wears her spiritual awareness as a badge of honour - and something to be proud of - rather than something to be embarrassed about.

In this instance, as a Level Five soul, Susan will openly acknowledge her spiritual interests to her friends without any shame and feel proud that she is such an enlightened soul. She may even encourage her friends to follow her lead and be willing to share everything she has learned.

This is the key difference between a Level Four soul and a Level Five soul. At Level Four we have suddenly been awakened to spiritual reality and we are struggling to come to terms with it or deal with it. But by Level Five the crisis is over and now this new knowledge and insight has been fully assimilated into the soul's life and no longer needs to be hidden from friends and family. A Level Five soul is happy to 'come out' and be proud of who they are.

A Stage Five soul, then, has resolved all the inner conflicts suffered as a Level Four soul and the dark night of the soul is now over and replaced by a new spiritual confidence. A newly emerged Level Five soul is ready and willing to face the challenges of this new level of soul development - whatever they might be. During this transitional period a number of behavioural and personality changes also accompany the soul on their onward journey. These personality changes are nearly always noticed by all those around them - particularly friends and family - and this can sometimes be a cause of conflict in relationships.

The shift in personality is marked by a number of things, but predominantly a shift in the soul's interests, pastimes, hobbies and ethics, which can change significantly. Let's look at a few examples of how these changes might manifest.

If the soul is in a career job, then the focus on the career may well shift dramatically as the soul starts to question the relevance of the job and the ethical and moral implications of the work being undertaken. The Level Five soul will suddenly start to take a huge interest in the overall goals of his or her employer and start asking questions about 'human rights, 'third world exploitation', 'pollution', 'deforestation', 'exploitation of natural resources', 'care of wildlife' and 'sexual equality' etc. Very often these questions arise only at Level Five because most Level Four souls are more focused on things like salary and career prospects than these deeper issues, but this is not always the case. There will always be some souls who are concerned about such issues at a much earlier stage of their journey. Every individual is different - and even Level One souls can be very aware of social injustices.

Level Five souls are also more inclined to become more conscious of their own mortality and start developing more of an interest in their personal soul journey. They start thinking about their life - and also all their previous lives in a wider and more spiritual context. They may even recognise what stage of the path they are on - more subconsciously than consciously - and may even take up the practice of meditation or mindfulness to see if it helps them gain greater insight.

At the same time, they become more conscious of their health and the subject of food and drink become more than just something on the weekly shopping list. Looking after the physical body as well as caring for the mind, the body and the spirit suddenly becomes more important, as does a balanced diet and better nutrition. Even though these things may never have been of much importance in the past - they are now of significant interest to a Level Five soul. This change in interest in health and nutrition is often more subconscious than conscious because the fifth level soul is now more attuned to spirit and more open to receiving information from the 'other side'. In the previous stages of development messages are also being sent frequently from the universe to the soul but these are rarely picked up.

This is because souls are all like radios that can pick up messages from the spirit world, but they need to be - literally - on the right frequency in order to receive these messages clearly. Lower vibration level souls who are more egoistic, sceptical and materialist tend to 'tune out' these unwanted frequencies because they are a challenge to their belief systems. But by Level Five the soul has become more receptive and subconsciously tuned their attention to these higher-level spiritual frequencies allowing messages to be received. These messages are never loud and clear but rather subtle and quiet so the listener needs to be attuned and receptive for the message to transmit smoothly from the 'transmitter' to the 'receiver'. Regular meditation practitioners are usually the first to start receiving these transmissions.

A Level Five soul does not just receive messages about health and nutrition though. This is just a typical example. By this stage of their development they are likely to be receiving messages on many different topics including guidance messages, warning messages and information messages. The Level Five soul will usually mistake most of these messages as intuition or gut instinct because the distinction between a spiritual message and a strong intuition are always very difficult to distinguish. Also, many of these messages may be missed because the soul is very new to this experience and not yet fully equipped to receive them. But slowly, over time, receptivity and awareness become stronger.

As these messages become more frequent, the Level Five soul might start to wonder where these messages are coming from, or to be more exact, they are becoming more curious about 'who' it is that is transmitting them.

The answer to this question is an important one. Psychics and Mediums usually say that they receive messages directly from the universe or the spirit world (the terms can be used interchangeably) and this is true. But the spirit world is very complex

- much more complex than the earthly realms - and messages can come from many sources. If, for example, a Psychic or Medium is giving one of their clients a spiritual reading it is usually because the client wants to contact deceased loved ones, relatives or friends. So, the Psychic will be listening or attuning specifically to particular souls who have transitioned to the other side.

This is a very different scenario from a soul who is still living on the Earth Plane and is receiving seemingly random messages at random times without the intervention of any Psychics or Mediums. In these instances, the messages are likely to come from two other sources but *not* (or very rarely) from deceased relatives or friends. The messages are most likely to emanate from the Level Five soul's Guardian Angel or Spirit Guides whose presence has already been described in Part One of this book. The reason that the messages come from the soul's Guardian Angel or Spirit Guides, rather than transitioned souls, are complex and described in more detail in the section on seventh level souls.

If you ever go to large bookshops where is a section called 'Mind, Body and Spirit' or 'Self-Help' and see people browsing the shelves they are quite likely to be souls between Level Four and Six and are therefore most likely to be within Stage Five of their spiritual development. That is because these are the souls that have become hungry for knowledge and want to supplement their natural spiritual development with more 'evidence' and wisdom. These are not the sort of books that are attractive to Stage One souls who would regard such books as "nonsense" and, strangely enough, Stage Seven souls also rarely browse these books, but for a different reason. It is because their spiritual wisdom has reached a level where they feel secure in their depth of knowledge and therefore find many of the books in these sections of a bookshop or library too basic or superfluous.

As the Level Five soul continues on their path, other aspects of their life will also be changing as will their attitudes and interests. The impasse of the Level Four experience has now dissipated, and the heart chakra has become more open and receptive. These changes will manifest in many different ways including having a greater compassion for all living things, as well as new interests in subjects like yoga, meditation, tai chi, reiki energy healing etcetera and it very likely that the Level Five soul will also want to attend a few courses or workshops on spiritual related subjects to make new friends and to acquire more knowledge. Life generally now has more meaning and is no longer random. A new child-like wonder about how the Universe works has also made life much more interesting.

In addition, the Level Five Soul will start to feel more energised and have more vitality than in previous Stages of their journey. They will have acquired more mental positivity and have a greater sense of wellbeing. They will feel more motivated to face up to life's daily challenges and start viewing their life as more of an exciting journey than the fighting to survive viewpoint of Level One souls.

Over the years a developing Level Five soul will have fully recovered from the crisis they lived through as a Level Four soul. Their spiritual development will have accelerated by leaps and bounds since then, and their awareness of their place in the universe will have become a lot clearer. When the time is right the universe will acknowledge their progress and then start to gently nudge them forward towards their next step of their journey.

The Fool has now met The Hierophant and has been taught about the true nature of the immortal soul and the true purpose of his or her journey. The difficulties of the past have now been left behind and The Fool is now moving forward with a newfound confidence and a growing spiritual awareness. The Hero has met with the Goddess and received her wisdom and guidance relating to the keys to enlightenment. She continues to be the Hero's guide on the next part of the journey now that many of the challenges and obstacles of the past have been overcome. The soul has now reached the Throat Chakra where the focus is on honest and open communication, connection to others, self-knowledge, spiritual growth, higher vibration thinking and synthesising new concepts and ideas.

Summary of Stage Five of the Soul's Path/ Characteristics of a Level Five soul

* The Level Five soul has finally comes to terms with who they really are.
* The Level Four 'crisis' is over.
* There is a new-found confidence: "Yes, I *am* a spiritual person...".
* The ego has now been subdued and recognised for what it is.
* A sense of calm and more acceptance that 'things are how they should be'.
* Open to spiritual guidance and new concepts/ ideas.
* Friends and family noticing the 'new personality'.

❊ Feeling ready to face the challenges of the spiritual path.

❊ Deeper thoughts about career/life-purpose/ethics/morality.

❊ No more fear of death. Acceptance of the immortal soul.

❊ New interests like yoga, meditation, tai chi, energy healing.

❊ More health awareness - nutrition/diet etc.

❊ More trusting of intuition.

❊ Heart is more 'open'/more compassionate.

❊ 'Life is an exciting journey'.

STAGE SIX

"Awakening is not changing who you are
but discarding who you are not".
Deepak Chopra

CHAKRA: SIX (LIGHT)

Sanskrit Name - 'Ajna'
Location - Centre of the forehead
Colour - Indigo
Common Name - 'Brow', 'Pineal' or 'Third Eye'
chakra
Characteristics - The focus is on seeing a deeper
reality i.e. seeing things on the inner and outer
planes, self-reflection, wisdom, psychic awareness,
spiritual awareness, seeing beyond the physical
world, intuition, inner knowing, discernment,
wisdom, living in the light.

Tarot Card: 'The Star'

The Fool, invigorated after his meeting with the wise
Hierophant, has continued on his soul journey and faced
all of his or her challenges and obstacles with a new sense
of determination and purpose. Now he has arrived at a
point where a bright star is hovering in the sky above his
head and a young woman has opened a large chest from
which many objects and strange creatures are pouring

out. In Tarot imagery the card called 'The Star' portrays Pandora opening the box containing the meaning, reality and knowledge of human life. The Fool watches as Pandora opens the box of secrets and mysteries and releases them. In this moment the childlike ignorance of The Fool is instantaneously replaced with deep wisdom about the true nature of life and our immortal soul. The Fool follows Pandora's upward gaze to the brilliant 'Star of Hope' twinkling above.

Hero's Journey: 'Atonement with Source'

The Goddess has now led the Hero on the next step of the journey away from the harsh realities and battles of the material world across another threshold and into a new mysterious world of spiritual reality. The Hero's initial confusion has now given way to an acceptance of who he or she is - as well as an acceptance of the existence of the spiritual realms. Now the Hero's challenge is to turn within and find the key to enlightenment by connecting to - and atoning with - the divine intelligence that is the 'Source' of all things and the mother of all souls.

The transition from Level Five to Level Six on the soul's journey is probably the most 'blurred' of all the transitions on the soul's journey because it is difficult to pinpoint the moment when the transition occurs. Sometimes it can take many years - but in some cases it can be less than one year. A Level Six soul knows without question that they are on a very important mission and their journey is of critical importance. They are fully aware that they are on the path and need to stay on the path. They are also fully aware that they have agreed to a Soul Contract prior to their present incarnation and need to fulfil that contract if they are to progress in their soul evolution and enjoy the benefits of that achievement in their next incarnation. So, the level of commitment to following the soul path is much higher for a Level Six soul than a Level Five soul.

The biggest issue that faces all Level Six souls though, is the frustration of knowing without doubt that they are here on the Earth Plane for a very important purpose - to fulfil their Soul Contract - but they still don't know what it is exactly that they have agreed to achieve within that contract or what they have signed up to! This statement, however, is not entirely true, because some Level Six souls, and indeed some Level Five souls too, *do* discover their purpose through various channels. But in general terms *most* Level Sixes still need to find their real purpose by accessing their Soul Contracts in order to discover what it is they need to achieve and learn - in this - their current incarnation.

But before we explore the issue of the Soul Contract in more depth let's first look at the typical characteristics of a Level Six soul and how it differs from their days spent at Level Five. One of the main spiritual changes a Level Six soul will typically experience is a marked increase in synchronicities!

Synchronicity is an interesting subject that could take a whole book to explain by itself. Synchronicities are *like* co-incidences (which we all experience) but they are *not* coincidences. Someone once said to me that a "Synchronicity is like a coincidence on steroids" and that's quite a good analogy. We all experience synchronicities during our life whether we are a Level One soul or Level Seven soul and it is true to say that the frequency of synchronicities escalates the further along the spiritual path we progress. At Level One on our journey we may get one or two significant synchronicities during the space of a year. By the time we reach Level Seven however, synchronicities are almost a daily occurrence and reality and eventually pile up on each other to such an extent that they just become a new normality and accepted for what they are.

So, why is this? Surely coincidences are just an unusual and inexplicable random event? Well, this simplistic Level One view of coincidences and synchronicities is actually flawed because no synchronicity is ever random as we will see when we discuss souls at Level Seven.

But for now, it is suffice to say that due to the way the universe works and the way the law of karma works, Level Six souls will soon have to get used to synchronicities being an increasingly common event in their lives. This is no bad thing though, for synchronicities are a way of the spirit world sending all of us subtle messages. Books fall off bookshelves in front of us that we should read, the people we are supposed to meet to aid us on our journey seem to turn up again and again in our life more frequently, potential life dangers are avoided intuitively and new opportunities open up unexpectedly that are perfectly in alignment for our onward soul progression. We all need to welcome synchronicities into our life more consciously rather than shrug them off as odd coincidences and nothing more.

So, the Level Six soul is now very focused on following his or her spiritual path with determination. They may not yet know the precise terms of the Soul Contract that they agreed to before this incarnation, but they are on a quest to find this out. Their feet are still in both camps in terms of living in both the everyday material world and the spiritual world simultaneously however, they still need to earn a living and attend to the challenges of real life even though they have a much greater awareness of the big picture in spiritual terms.

In this frame of mind Level Sixes are also learning to open up their mind to a much greater extent. It could be said that soul development can be evidenced by being correlated directly with what we call open-mindedness. In this context a Level One low vibration soul is spiritually closed minded and a Level Seven high vibration soul is spiritually totally open minded and all the other souls are somewhere on the sliding scale between one to seven.

So, by Level Six, most souls are becoming increasingly open-minded about the world they live in. They are now looking at day-to-day world events through a much wider lens than simply accepting what they read in the newspapers or watch on TV. They are starting to make their own judgements about what is happening in the world from not just a global perspective but also from a spiritual and universal perspective and they are now seeing things not just from a deeper moral and ethical standpoint but also in the context of much wider time horizons. Their intuition is now much sharper and there is also, therefore, a much greater appreciation of the interconnectedness between things. Their awareness of the 'bigger picture' enables them to spot links between events or global issues that might seem disconnected to others.

For example, an immature soul at Level One, who might be an investor, might look at investments from the view of short term profit only, and disregard the deeper underlying issues of whether the organisation he or she is investing in is contributing to protecting the planet or exploiting it. To a Level One soul - or Level Two soul - profit is the primary goal of investing. But for a Level Six soul, who may also be an investor, their moral and ethical beliefs are now aligned with a higher purpose so that investing in anything that harms people or the environment is no longer an option. This is because as souls learn and grow through each stage of their journey their values, morals and ethics change and subconsciously become aligned with more long-term planetary and spiritual goals. Their comprehension of Planet Earth is no longer about a spinning lump of rock in a chaotic and random universe but of a living, breathing conscious entity vibrating at a specific frequency and nurturing an interconnected web of life.

At Level Six, souls will also be experiencing other changes of character, just as they did as a Stage Five soul.

They will be looking at their material surroundings - meaning their home and their possessions - in a new way and receiving intuitions about wanting to change things. They may get sudden urges to clean their home more thoroughly or to start de-cluttering and throwing out lots of old or unwanted possessions. They feel a need to get rid of everything superfluous or throw out things they no longer need. They want the rooms they live in to be full of more space and less clutter. There may even be a sense of possessions weighing them down. Now that their spiritual mission has become so central to their lives all this other material 'stuff' is somehow getting in the way and needs to be discarded. It is probably true to say that the further along the path a soul moves the more their material possessions are discarded. There is an inner intuition and awareness that the less we own the more freedom we have to follow our true path. As said before, the only thing we carry from one incarnation to the next is our immortal soul which holds within it our unique personality and our karmic record. We don't take - or need - anything else.

There is another element to this change of behaviour that also needs to be mentioned and that is to do with energies. Advanced souls have the ability to sense the energies inherent within objects because, although mainstream scientists would still disagree, all objects are infused with energy that can be intuitively sensed by all advanced souls. This means that everyday objects that are handled frequently by their owners start to absorb the energy of their owners. (This is not true of newly manufactured objects however, because the energies of the owner need time to be absorbed into the objects).

This is why people who are 'sensitives' (and they can be anywhere on the soul journey spectrum) can pick up a random object from a second-hand shop, charity shop, boot fair or garage sale etc and sense the energy of the object, or more precisely, the energy of the previous owner or owners. And this energy can range from extremely positive to extremely negative. This is why most people will intuitively pick up an object before choosing to buy it. They may believe that they are examining the object through sight, sound, touch and smell, only because they are unaware that their 'sixth sense' is also being used to make the buying decision too. If the object exudes a very positive energy, then you are more likely to buy it than if it exudes a negative energy. But this is not usually done consciously, unless you are a Seventh Level soul. For most people, to buy or not to buy is based primarily on what is *subconsciously* experienced when holding the object. Things like second-hand jewellery and second-hand clothes are the most energetically infused, followed by things like books, vinyl records, ornaments, framed photographs etcetera. Other things that have been previously owned but not touched or held as often, (like domestic appliances, furniture, garden tools etcetera) are less infused with energies and are thus more neutral.

Sixth Level souls will have acquired this skill to a certain degree and, as well as sensing the positive or negative energies of objects, will also be attracted to surround themselves with things that energise and uplift them. These will typically be objects like natural crystals, running water features (indoor or outdoor fountains for example), wind chimes, naturally scented candles, essential oils, uplifting posters and pictures with nature themes or with inspirational quotes or small objects that give them pleasure (flowers, feathers, fossils, rocks, shells, natural wood, leaves etc).

If you visit someone's home and it is filled with these kinds of objects, then it is quite likely that it is the home of a soul in the Five to Seven range of development. So, although the soul at this level will be throwing out a lot of material possessions and de-cluttering, they will often be replacing the discarded and no longer wanted things with the more inspirational and energising objects described above.

Also, in addition to a greater sensitivity towards objects, Level Six souls will have also developed a greater sensitivity towards people. Up until now, judgements about other people will have been based predominantly on what is picked up by the five senses. But now the so-called sixth sense comes more into play and the sixth level soul will be intuitively and subconsciously sensing peoples' true colours. Very quickly a sixth level soul will instinctively sense - and be drawn to - the people they want to be friends with and close to (i.e. mostly other souls who are at, or near, to the same level of soul maturity) and they will also recognise those whom they want to avoid or spend less time with.

All souls exude energy because we are all energetic, electrical and bio-chemical entities at the cellular level. And subconsciously we pick up these energetic signals which contain a lot of information at subtle frequency levels. So, the reality for all souls at all levels of maturity is that when we meet people, whether they are friends or strangers, most of what we pick up about them is at the subconscious and vibratory level.

There are certain categories of people - and we have all met them - who can be termed 'Energy Vampires'. We recognise these people as being such because, after spending time in their company, we always feel energetically drained after they have left. It needs to be made clear though, that energy vampires are not evil or nasty people. They may be very normal at the superficial level and they usually have no idea that they are energy vampires. But there is something about their personality that has a draining effect on other people. This subject would take another whole book to explain but in simple terms when we feel that our normally vibrant energy has been sucked dry after meeting certain individuals, this is actually a true description of what has happened. People who are energy vampires have depleted energy levels for psychological or physical reasons and therefore need to supplement their lost natural energy by 'feeding' on the energy of other more healthy individuals in order to maintain their strength. And, for all energy vampires, souls who are at the Fifth, Sixth or Seventh levels offer them a veritable feast because these souls have the strongest and purest energy to feed on. Energy vampires are never consciously aware that they are feeding on their friend's or relative's positive energies and never do it maliciously. But advanced souls recognise instinctively which of their friends and acquaintances are energy vampires and gradually start distancing themselves from these people and spending more time with like-minded souls who exude more positive energies.

This is why another strong characteristic of Level Six souls is that they gradually start to move away from their old circle of friends to form new relationships with those whom they are more spiritually attuned to. They also have a need to leave behind everything that is deemed to be a negative influence on their life and start to gravitate towards everything that is positive.

Another characteristic of developing souls that is often, but not always, manifested is a change in their musical tastes. Over many years - and on our journey through life - it is quite likely that our musical tastes and preferences will change as we ourselves change and this is quite normal. Very often though, and particularly for Level Five, Six and Seven souls, a growing interest in what might be termed spiritual music is experienced. This might be devotional music, chanting, soft melodic relaxation and meditative music or specific classical pieces that have an uplifting effect on the listener. Songs that were loved years ago may no longer have the same effect on the listener, while new types of music that were previously ignored now seem more attractive and melodious.

Similarly, Level Six souls are also becoming more aware of not just the power inherent in spiritual music but also the inherent power of words. This is because all music, words, sounds and frequencies contain a quality that is deeper than their surface expression - as well as their own negative or positive energies. Indigenous tribes, Shamans and Poets have known about this instinctively for countless centuries but in our more sanitised and technological world this knowledge has been lost. A Sixth Level soul has rediscovered this truth and now chooses his or her words much more carefully and their language patterns may therefore change.

We saw earlier how swearing and bad or offensive language - which carry negative frequencies - is generally more prevalent in Level One souls. By the time a soul has evolved to Level Six, words that carry negative frequencies are subconsciously avoided in preference of words that carry only positive frequencies.

Level Six souls still struggle to be both spiritual and practical simultaneously however, and because of this they are likely to be increasingly confused about their place in society. They will start to feel like an 'odd one out' because they are steadily losing interest in the mainstream media, mainstream TV, bland music, social media, celebrity news or anything else that is superficial or trivial. At the same time, their interests are widening, and they are seeking out more books or high-quality documentaries about subjects like reincarnation, karma, meditation, holistic health, healthy eating and energy healing. It is likely they will have also acquired more concern for human and animal rights and the need to maintain a sustainable planet.

Being in nature, whether walking in natural forests or along the sea shore - or even spending time in wild remote places is also preferred to being in crowded urban spaces. The Level Six soul is now much more attracted to the frequencies emitted by the natural world and is more sensitive to the harmful effects of man-made frequencies that saturate our cities and towns.

Their fear of death has now dissipated completely as their awareness of their true identity as an immortal soul has become a certainty and, in relation to this awareness, they start recognising issues within their current lifestyle that need fixing. Level Six souls also tend to start seeking more solitude than before, are drawn to more gentle people, and start seeking more personal independence - no longer wanting to conform to societal norms that seem unfair, unjust or unethical. They may even want to join or start up pressure groups and campaigns relating to issues they feel passionately about.

These new interests and changing characteristics are all related to an increasing need for some kind of purification and detoxing. These feelings are all completely natural symptoms of spiritual growth and, although Level Six souls may not be consciously aware of the physical, mental and spiritual changes they are going through, their subconscious is carefully preparing them for their next step on their soul's journey.

The Fool has witnessed Pandora opening the box of secrets and has now attained a deep wisdom about the true nature of life and the immortal soul. His or her life and spiritual journey have now become the Fool's prime objective. The Hero's physical challenges have now been overcome and it is to now time to turn within and find the key to enlightenment by connecting to the divine intelligence that is the source of all things and the mother of all souls. The Soul, having ascended to the Third Eye chakra is now able to see a deeper reality beyond the physical world that is defined by intuition, inner knowing, discernment, wisdom, living in the light, compassion and truth.

Summary of Stage Six of the Soul's Path/ Characteristics of a Stage Six soul

* Full awareness of the implications of their spiritual journey.
* Ready to face up to all the challenges of their soul contract.
* More synchronicities happening and becoming the new 'normality'.
* Changing lifestyle and changing interests.
* Changing circle of friends and avoiding energy vampires .
* Looking deeper into world issues rather than just accepting media news.
* Awareness of the world as a living organism needing care.
* Less interested in material things - discarding unnecessary possessions.
* De-cluttering - picking up energetic sensitivity to objects.
* Attraction to things like crystals, scented candles, inspirational images, running water

features, fossils, rocks, feathers, flowers, wind chimes, shells, leaves etc..

* Wider moral/ethical worldview.
* More awareness of the interconnectedness of all things.
* More developed intuition.
* Desire to spend more time in nature.
* Less ego.
* Change in musical tastes to different frequencies.
* Awareness of the power and energy of words and sounds.
* Full acceptance of death as merely a transition.

STAGE SEVEN

"Learn to get in touch with the silence within yourself and know that everything in this life has a purpose. There are no mistakes, no coincidences. All events are blessings given to us to learn from".
Elizabeth Kübler-Ross

CHAKRA: SEVEN (THOUGHT)

Sanskrit Name - 'Sahasrara'
Location - Top of the skull
Colour - Violet
Common Name - 'Crown' chakra
Characteristics - The focus is on connection to Source or divine intelligence, cosmic (or 'unity') consciousness, ultimate liberation from body consciousness to spirit consciousness, liberation from karmic bonds, serenity, oneness, bliss and enlightenment.

Tarot Card: 'The World'

The Fool has completed the first part of his journey and successfully navigated the soul path from ignorance to spiritual maturity. But this is only the journey of one incarnation. The next part of the journey is the transition from the earthly realm to the spiritual realm before the next rebirth becomes necessary. In Tarot imagery 'The World' card depicts a snake with the end of its tail in its mouth creating a perfect circle - the representation of the endless cycle of death and rebirth as well as 'Nature' and 'Source'. In the centre of the circle is an androgynous figure representing the union of the masculine and feminine aspects of duality and balance. Overall the card stands for achievement and integration. The completion of a quest and the receiving of wisdom. The journey is over and the rewards of enlightenment are waiting.

Hero's Journey: 'The Master of Two Worlds'

The Hero has finally returned from the journey and the adventure and the quest is over. The Hero has met all the challenges and defeated the tyranny of the ego. It is time to return home and rest. But now 'home' is very different from when the journey started. Everything has somehow changed and it is no longer as it was. Or maybe it is because the Hero has changed and now sees his or her 'home' with new eyes. The third-eye has been opened and visions of eternity, purity and immortality have replaced the earlier certainties built of scepticism, arrogance and ignorance. The challenges of the Earth Plane are now recognised for what they really are and the awareness of the Spiritual Realms are now also recognised and embraced. The Hero is now 'Master of Two Worlds'. The Hero's journey on the Earth plane is coming to a close. But now a new journey beckons; the journey back to Source.

And now, finally, we have arrived at Level Seven of the soul's journey. To have come this far a soul has truly had to work hard to face up to so many challenges. Not just in this life but for hundreds, maybe thousands of lives and even now it's not the end. Now it is just another temporary resting place before the next life calls us back to face more important tasks that have yet to be completed before we can finally return to Source.

"The souls of people on their way to Earth-life pass through a room full of lights. Each one takes a taper, often only a spark, to guide it in the dim country of this world. But some souls, by rare fortune, are detained longer and have time to grasp a handful of tapers, which they weave into a torch. These are the torch-bearers of humanity - its poets, seers and saints who lead and lift the race out of darkness, towards the light. They are the law-givers and saviours, the light-bringers, way-showers and truth-tellers, and without them, humanity would lose its way in the dark".
Plato

The perpetual cycle of transition and rebirth means that for the Seventh Level soul, yet another life is on the horizon, with new challenges and lessons still to be learned. For even those at Stage Seven have not yet reached the end of the path. Another new life is already calling and another new-born is waiting for our soul to accompany it on its journey. For Buddhists the world over, this means yet another round of suffering before Nirvana is finally reached - the 'final lifetime' before the physical body can at last be discarded and the now purified and enlightened soul can finally return 'Home' forever. The time will have come for the soul to return at last to the Source from which it first came. There is no longer any need to adopt a physical form or to face any more challenges and obstacles. Now is the ultimate joyous moment of being finally reunited with soul mates and the greatest light of all - the Source from which everything first emanated - whichever name you choose to call it.

A soul that has managed to navigate the long path through many incarnations from Stage One through to Stage Six has acquired an incredible amount of wisdom and knowledge on this arduous journey. And now, finally, the time has come to experience the challenges of the final stage on the path - Stage Seven.

So, what are the typical characteristics of a Stage Seven soul? How are they different from a Level Six soul? And how do they manifest? Let's take a look and examine some of the typical attributes of a Stage Seven soul...

During our own lifetimes we may well have met people who are living in this seventh state of existence. It's also possible we may have intuitively sensed this if we are ourselves are somewhere between Stage Five and Stage Seven. (Even those at Stage One can sometimes be intuitive enough to pick up some of the attributes of a soul at the seventh stage because of the energies they exude or the colour and energy of their aura).

A typical Stage Seven soul will have many specific characteristics and attributes. Some characteristics will be similar to Stage Six souls - but there are also many other characteristics that are usually only manifested at Stage Seven.

One characteristic that is very common to all souls at Level Seven is the desire to not hurt any living thing - whether it be plant, animal or insect. Stage Seven souls feel a very strong connection to all living things at the cellular level and may even feel able to communicate at a rudimentary level with all life forms. The thought of deliberately hurting or killing any form of life is abhorrent to a seventh level soul and this feeling ranges from a human being down to the smallest insect. Seventh level souls have a deep respect for all life forms and believe that every life form has an inherent right to live. The very thought of causing harm to a creature that has been created by Source is horrific to a seventh level soul who believes that ALL life is sacred and should be protected. The hunting of any animals for sport sickens seventh level souls to the core of their being. Even picking a flower can cause a tear to be shed such is their sensitivity.

Similarly, news media that report atrocities and wars including genocide, rape, torture or human rights violations make seventh level souls openly weep. The feelings of compassion and sympathy are often too much for them to bear and many souls at this level will often go somewhere quiet and secluded to grieve and recover alone. They very often feel the pain of those who are suffering in a very real and almost tangible way and may even display similar symptoms of someone undergoing severe trauma as if they were vibrating in sympathy.

Seventh level souls also tend to display an increased childlike fascination and awareness of natural beauty including things like clouds, leaves, butterflies, running water and trees etcetera. Being immersed in nature is a 'transcendental experience' for souls at this level. The natural world of rivers, waterfalls, mountains and forests brings them huge joy and energises their bodies and minds. And this is not just about an appreciation of natural beauty. It is much more than that. Seventh level souls are actually able to *feel* the real energies emanating from nature. They can feel the energy of the negative ions being released by waterfalls at a cellular level and they can also feel and sense the natural chemical scents exuded from trees and plants.

For Seventh level souls, nature is not just a beautiful expression of Source but is also a healer at the quantum level. By the time a soul has reached Level Seven, 'ego-consciousness' has been replaced by 'eco-consciousness'. And, unlike most Level One souls who see nature as something to be freely exploited for mankind's benefit, Level Seven souls put nature above ego and see it as something to be protected, respected and nurtured. Even the sight of a tree being cut down can hurt a seventh level soul to their core.

Being in a large city, by way of contrast, causes them huge distress and discomfort so seventh level souls have a physical *need* to be immersed in nature because the natural world rejuvenates and energises their mental and physical welfare. A city or large town is buzzing with both the 'emotional frequencies' of many hundreds of stressed souls as well as the buzzing of life-draining electromagnetic pollution exuded by telephone masts, WiFi, electricity cables and computers etc. Being surrounded by unnatural man-made frequencies can completely drain a Level Seven soul's energy and it may take them a long time to recuperate.

Level Seven souls also live with a perpetual and constant feeling of 'Gratitude'. This is not the same thing as the feeling we all experience when friends and relatives kindly present us with a gift on our birthday or at Christmas - which is fleeting and temporary. For a seventh level soul this feeling of gratitude is constant, and it is always there. It is difficult to describe in human terms, but it is best described as an internal warm feeling that generates a message back to Source many times a day. It is a simple 'Thank You' message that is expressing gratitude just for being alive. It is a subliminal, psychic and telepathic message from a seventh level soul back to Source that says something like "Thank you for this life. Thank you for this opportunity to express and manifest my potential. Thank you for caring for me and nurturing me." In some cases, this expression of gratitude is felt so powerfully that some souls like to communicate directly with every one of the fifty trillion cells in their own body expressing gratitude for all the unconditional love that each bodily cell contributes to keeping the body functioning at optimum level and bringing them health and vitality.

Another common characteristic of seventh level souls is their ability to grant true forgiveness to everyone who has wronged them. Throughout our lives we have all interacted with people who have taken advantage of us. They may have borrowed money from us or borrowed our possessions and never repaid us or never returned what is rightfully ours. Or they may just be frustrated lower level souls looking for someone to blame for their own problems. This abuse of a Level Seven soul's kind nature upsets them deeply and each soul may react in different ways. Sometimes, lower level souls react aggressively and demand what they are due, or constantly moan about how unfairly they have been treated. But souls at the seventh level find it very difficult to be assertive in these circumstances. There is something inherent in their makeup which causes them to simply forgive. A seventh level soul's philosophy is to recognise and respect souls who are operating at a lower level of maturity and understand that they are also learning lessons at their own pace which cannot be, and should not be, accelerated.

This means that if someone at a lower level on the soul path refuses or forgets to repay a debt or return something loaned, the seventh level soul will simply accept this as an attribute of the other soul that is indicative of their soul maturity and forgive their oversight or lack of acknowledgement or cooperation. Seventh level souls always look at the bigger picture and think in cosmic timescales. A single life is but a fleeting moment for a mature seventh level soul so forgiveness is always a more preferable solution than seeking revenge or justice. Those below Level Seven find it hard to understand this philosophy and believe assertiveness is a more appropriate solution for people who have 'wronged' them, but Level Seven souls are willing to let it go because their eyes are fixed on much wider horizons both spatially and temporally.

As Wendy Kennedy eloquently explains in her book about soul evolution:

"As you reach this elevated level of awareness, you will find that you may observe others' behaviour as being of a lower vibrational nature, but you are unaffected by it and simply observe it. You do not judge it as being right or wrong, but rather see it as an interesting vibrational selection and hold compassion for them as they move along their path".
("The Great Human Potential" by Tom Kenyon and Wendy Kennedy)

In the earlier description of souls at Level Six I described how the spiritual journey and the soul's path had become an increasingly important element in their life and was becoming a gradually more dominant force steering their decisions and actions. By the time a soul reaches Level Seven however, this 'dominant steering force' has now become the most overriding influence of their entire life and *everything* else is now considered 'secondary'.

This means that for a seventh level soul, to follow their spiritual path is now their *prime reason for existence*. Their onward journey on the Earth Plane is entirely defined by their Soul Contract and this mission now takes precedence over every other decision and choice they have to make in life. Their contract and their mission has now become the moral and spiritual compass by which they steer their whole life and meeting their spiritual goals has become the prime driving force that motivates them. Fears and concerns in the material world no longer hold any great significance for them and the Spirit World is now more real and tangible than the material world they have experienced thus far. Their entire focus has now shifted irretrievably towards seeking the light that emanates from Source and they also have an increasing sense of nostalgia for their previous pre-birth existence in the spiritual realms. They feel ready to 'go Home' whenever they are privileged enough to be called.

This does not mean that Seventh level souls blatantly ignore the material world though. They are still aware of the need to be able to function on the Earth Plane and in everyday life, but it is becoming increasingly difficult for them to do so. This is because they have a deep subconscious and conscious awareness of the true nature of reality and can see beneath the surface of most situations, relationships and conflicts including major world events.

Seventh Level souls don't tend to use the TV or newspapers or popular media to gain information like souls at the lower levels. They have developed a much deeper intuitive knowledge about what is really going on in the world. Things like wars, conflict, environmental exploitation, social injustice, pollution, deforestation or cruelty to any living creature is abhorrent to them and they can immediately sense the deeper ego-driven motives that cause lower level souls to inflict damage to the planet and to their fellow human beings.

Seventh level souls feel hugely saddened by 'man's inhumanity to man' because there is nothing in their own nature that equates to the motives of these immature souls. They realise and accept that these immature souls are all on their own individual journeys and that the law of karma will ultimately bring them to a recognition of the error of their ways. But this also means that Seventh level souls often feel powerless to stop these atrocities because the souls committing them are rarely open to listening to the wisdom of more mature souls. Immature souls make decisions that are both ego-based and fear-based and this is a dangerous combination. Most conflict, on the scale from small domestic disagreements right up to world wars, emanate primarily from the need to protect the ego and the reaction to 'fear'. Only when both of these elements can be mastered internally will peace spread faster than conflict. Seventh level souls now know this intuitively and try their best to persuade others to accept this fundamental truth but they are rarely listened to. When a high vibration soul tries to communicate with a low vibration soul the vibrational gap is usually too wide to be bridged.

The only tools that a seventh level soul can use to combat these injustices is by spreading true and unconditional love as widely as possible to as many individuals as possible and by spreading awareness of the true nature of the soul through sharing wisdom - and teaching the principles of unity consciousness and compassion - to all souls who are willing to listen.

Unity consciousness is essentially the ultimate solution for all souls seeking the answer to solving the world's greatest problems because it refers to the recognition that everything on the whole planet and indeed the whole universe is intimately and energetically connected. The illusion of separation is thus recognised as the cause of all hurt and conflict in the world for the simple reason that mankind is unaware of his or her intrinsic connection to all things. So millions of low vibration immature souls continue to inflict hurt on other souls blissfully unaware that the hurt being caused will only reflect straight back at them and keep them in bondage to their own egos.

All mature or 'Old Souls' know that when they are in the spirit world there is no 'us and them' and there is no 'me and other'. Our energetic, vibrational and quantum connection to everything else in the entire universe is a universal truth that has been present since time began and is what is known as an immutable law.

In real world terms this means if we hurt someone, we are actually hurting ourselves too. If we exploit the planet, we are exploiting ourselves too. If we spread negativity our own body becomes full of negativity. If we are unkind to someone, then we are being unkind to ourselves too. In the worst scenario, if we take someone's life deliberately then we are simultaneously not only killing millions of our *own* body cells (which effectively commit suicide in sympathy with the victim's cells) but we are also damaging our soul consciousness and our karmic record. In many cases of Post Traumatic Stress Disorder (PTSD) the act of killing someone has a direct effect on millions of the perpetrator's own body cells which still remains a medically unrecognised side-effect by the military.

The solution to stopping all world conflict, from the spiritual perspective, is simply to recognise the truth of unity consciousness. Because, if there is no 'other' and we are all 'one' then conflict is by definition and pure logic - completely pointless. Seventh Level souls know this intuitively and instinctively but have also been taught this universal truth by their spirit guides. But knowing this truth is a huge burden for any Seventh level soul living on the Earth Plane. This is because they can not only see through all of the injustices and wrong-doings of mankind, but they also understand the root causes of these things. The problem for seventh level souls is how to awaken all the lower level souls to the truth of unity consciousness in order to find a resolution.

That is why Seventh level souls often feel a compulsion to help other souls on their journey in any way they can, however small. This is because they still have a deep love for ALL souls - wherever they may be on their individual paths - and a deep compassion for anyone who is suffering.

But this burden of spiritual knowledge and awareness is very tough to live with on the Earth Plane, so seventh level souls tend to need long periods of solitude and silence to recharge their internal batteries. Rather than traditional holidays, which they may have enjoyed in earlier years, seventh level souls will now be drawn to get away to a different type of break or holiday which might be a yoga retreat or a meditation retreat which requires some time spent alone in uplifting natural surroundings and provides a chance to reconnect to their origins. It also provides time and space to connect with other like-minded souls near to, or at the seventh level.

Seventh level souls are conscious of the fact they are 'Lightworkers'. All souls, wherever they are on their soul journey, are potential lightworkers but are not always consciously aware of the fact. Being a lightworker, but not being aware of it consciously, can be a very painful place to be. This is because of the subconscious feelings that being a lightworker generates within us. When we sense these feelings and *know* we are a lightworker it is much easier to cope with. When we have these feelings but can't process them it can lead to deep depression and confusion sometimes leading to addictive behaviours.

Lightworkers are evolved souls who have come voluntarily to the Earth Plane to help heal the planet and heal all souls who feel lost or confused. They are our Earth Plane guides and mentors. They are the gentle spiritual people we meet from time to time on our life journey who speak from a place of wisdom and compassion. They inspire us and motivate us to see the bigger picture and lead our lives in a more spiritual way.

Seventh level souls will, by this stage of their soul journey, have no fear of death as they recognise death for what it really is. It is merely a transition point and does not need to be feared but rather welcomed. It is an opportunity for deep rest and to be reunited with their oldest friends - their 'Soul Group'. A seventh level soul knows that death is not the opposite of life as many lower level souls believe, rather it is the opposite of 'birth' - and birth is the greatest privilege the universe can bestow on a soul because it is the doorway into the most incredible experience possible.

This deep knowledge and wisdom that a seventh level soul has accrued over many lifetimes still makes it difficult for them to deal with the challenges and obstacles of living on the Earth Plane so there is a deep need to spend time with other enlightened souls. This means that by the time a soul has reached Stage Seven of their journey it will want to seek out others who are at the same level. Although still having a deep love and respect for all souls on the path, a seventh level soul will want to spend most of his or her time with other seventh level souls. And, as has been mentioned before, this can put a strain on relationships because although souls at different levels can marry or live together happily for many years there will come a time when the mis-match of soul levels can lead to conflict, upset and even separation or divorce. Although this is not always the case, it is unfortunately very common and remains a significant, but usually unacknowledged, cause of many breakups.

Seventh level souls will have gained a strong inner confidence whilst on their soul journey and they fear no-one. They are comfortable in their own body and will have great clarity in their mind including a deep sense of connection with the whole universe as well as compassion and love for all other souls. Many seventh level souls will enjoy regular meditation and the health and mental benefits that regular meditation provides as well as a deeper appreciation of 'sound' in terms of recognising the healing qualities of sound as a therapy and the spiritual connection that chanting with like-minded souls can bring. They will have learned intuitively how to look after themselves mentally and physically and may adopt specific practices that they enjoy like yoga, Tai Chi or slow, deep breathing exercises.

In terms of their homes, the majority of seventh level souls will tend to surround themselves with beautiful things (crystals, scented candles, uplifting music, inspirational words and pictures with meanings or beauty) following on from their attraction to these things at Level Six and will discard anything distasteful or which holds negative energies. Sensing 'energies' (a skill known as 'psychometry') has now become a normal and accepted part of everyday life for the average seventh level soul. This includes both the energy of objects and people, but also more sensitivity to other energies like electromagnetic radiation, electricity and even the energetic frequencies emanated by nature in general.

This ability, although available to all human beings and their souls, does not always manifest until later on their soul path and may not truly flower until levels six or seven. Similarly, Level Six and Level Seven souls are usually more aware of their own internal energies, their aura and their chakras and use these feelings to assess intuitively their own state of health. Many start to take an interest in the whole subject of energy healing and some choose to become trained as 'Reiki' healers or other forms of energy healers. They are also able to hold crystals and sense the different energy flows emanating from within different types of crystals.

Another fairly common trait of Level Seven souls is that they generally refuse to take any form of prescribed medication because they intuitively know how to heal themselves and can do this best when no extraneous chemicals are introduced into their body from mainstream medications. They trust the innate intelligence of their own cells to deal with and heal any health issues and also focus on maintaining their natural life energy by avoiding people or places that exude harmful negative energies.

Level Seven souls are acutely sensitive of their own internal feelings and energies and will be more consciously aware that they have a number of auric fields around their body. Some will actually start to 'see' other people's etheric and auric colour energy fields although this is generally quite a rare skill. Equally, they will be much more aware of their chakras and will sense the vibratory 'flow' of all their chakra points including not just their seven major chakras but also their secondary chakras, meridians and possibly the circular flows of the 'Ida' and 'Pingala' energy flow systems that also energise the body. Over time this extra-sensory awareness of all the energy flows within their body becomes so strong that Level Seven souls can intuitively sense their own state of health quite accurately and can often fix their own health issues by meditating and focusing positive energy onto anywhere in the body they feel discomfort or pain. Some Level Seven souls are able to self-diagnose and self-heal very effectively and many of them have lost faith in what might be termed traditional healthcare.

Some, but not all, seventh level souls can sometimes suffer symptoms like dizziness, nausea, tinnitus or other types of buzzing noises in the head which they may wrongly diagnose as a physical health problem. According to many spirit guides who have been contacted by seventh level souls about this subject, there is nothing to be feared from these feelings which are not actually caused by any physical ailment - but instead it is something that has been spiritually induced. According to these spirit guides there is sometimes a need to 'upgrade' an individual's vibration level from one level to another level in order to prepare them for a specific transition point. This is particularly common for Level Six souls who are desirous of progressing to Level Seven. For reasons which spirit guides tell us are difficult to explain, there are certain times when both our physical bodies and our energetic bodies need re-tuning or 'upgrading' to a slightly higher frequency of vibration in order to prepare us for transition from one soul level to the next.

There are many other traits or characteristics that mark a seventh level soul and their progress on the path. Their spiritual knowledge has been steadily increasing over many lifetimes and is now the core of who they are. They have transitioned from being spiritually aware Level Five and Six souls to fully fledged Level Seven souls and now spiritual *awareness* has been replaced by spiritual *certainty*. They now live their lives more in a way that is totally spiritually focused which makes navigating the 'real' world of the Earth Plane much more difficult than in previous lives. Being a seventh level soul in a crowd full of Level One or Level Two souls can be a very uncomfortable, lonely and scary place.

Being aware of the true nature of who they are, added to the pressures of trying to fulfil the goals of their soul contract, make some decisions more difficult to make for seventh level souls. They are increasingly aware of the strange feelings of being a spiritual being who is shackled to the dense matter of an earthly body. Which is, in fact, exactly what they are. But as well as having to accept this temporary limitation of being encased in a physical body there is a deep desire to do the 'right things' to stay on the path. But trying to plan a way forward through life and simultaneously hoping that every decision made is the right one can be extremely difficult. Seventh level souls are still human and they still make mistakes. As Helen Greaves so aptly sums it up:

"When in the body one is so limited by environment, emotions, difficulties, that it is very hard to judge accurately such results as might possibly ensue from the planning, and when we do try to assess the value, we are so often wrong because we ourselves - our small egotistic selves - get in the way and deflect the purpose". (*Helen Greaves – "Testimony of Light"*)

The philosophy of a seventh level soul has changed enormously over their soul evolution and over many lifetimes, the cynicism, disbelief and scepticism of a Level One soul has steadily matured into the unity consciousness awareness of a Level Seven soul. There is an acceptance that, 'everything is okay and is just how it is meant to be' and 'the universe will provide'. There is a constant heightened intuition about everything, less worry about trivial things and less interest in money or material acquisitions. A Level Seven soul is now living life as a consciously aware immortal spirit that now has to deal with the never-ending challenges and obstacles of the Earth Plane.

Their mindset has now started to shift from being a mere observer of lower level souls into a more compassionate position. They now have a burning desire to help and assist their fellow soul travellers on their journeys on the soul path. They feel a compulsion to rescue the lost, confused, angry or misguided souls that are struggling to find their way in an increasingly difficult world and to get them back on the right path. They feel a need to help these bewildered souls navigate and understand the true nature of their being and their destiny just as they themselves were helped in the early stages of their own journey. There is a clear realisation that lower level souls who have little or no conception of immortality, or the true nature of the soul, are driven by their emotions and ego-based logic which inevitably causes much anger, frustration and jealousy resulting in misguided actions that are often regretted later.

A seventh level soul, in contrast, has learned to live their life through consciousness and conscious awareness rather than through emotional reaction. This insight and 'way of being' perfectly enables them to help others who are yet to discover this revelation. A seventh level soul has developed to such a level of maturity that they become, in essence, a soul-infused personality as their awareness of their true nature now drives everything in their life including every decision they make. And this help is not just delivered by seventh souls to the immature souls. There is always another huge source of help and assistance that comes directly from the spirit world itself.

This help and assistance from the spirit world, which increases over time, enables seventh level souls to totally put their trust in their own intuition - and more than anything else this is probably the biggest single distinguishing factor between a level seven soul and a level six soul. This is effectively the 'golden key' that only a Level Seven soul has the capacity to turn in the lock. Only at level seven can a soul truly silence the ego and instead put total and complete trust in the universe. They have learned how to finally let the 'heart' overrule the 'head' which, for most of us, is the most difficult challenge we face on the Earth Plane.

What this means is that a mature level seven soul no longer has to agonise over making tough life decisions or worry about things that 'might happen'. They no longer have to think of situations in terms of having a Plan A or Plan B or a contingency plan if things go wrong. By putting one hundred percent trust in the universe they are effectively handing over control of their fate or destiny to the the spirit world and their guides. They know intuitively and with total certainty that they are exactly where they are supposed to be on their life journey, they know their mission and purpose, they accept transition as the natural course of existence and they have learned how to love their own immortal soul. There is no longer any shred of 'fear' or doubt about anything and they are happy to 'let go' and just 'be'. When this state of being becomes normality it is almost like living constantly in a state of bliss. This does not mean that life's daily challenges and frustrations have gone away though. They will always be present. It just means that these things no longer lead to feelings of anxiety or distress. They are simply accepted for what they are.

Level Seven souls are those people we occasionally meet who seem to effortlessly float along through life with serenity and at peace with themselves and everyone around them. They always seem to have a smile on their face and appear to be worry-free and relaxed. They never bother to fret over trivial issues or forcefully want to share their points of view. They accept people and situations for what they are without criticism or judgement and most of all they just seem to be enjoying 'life' in all its shades of complexity. Level Seven souls are more concerned with 'being' than 'doing'.

Another of the most distinguishing characteristics between a Level Six soul and a Level Seven soul is that a seventh level soul has a much greater awareness of the closeness of the spirit world, their spirit guides and in particular their own Guardian Angel. A vague awareness has existed for some time, but now the relationship between the Level Seven soul and their personal Guardian Angel is much more highly developed and they have become more like twins that are able to communicate telepathically. The Guardian Angel has been there all along of course - but only in the background, willing the soul they have watched over since birth to grow, learn and flourish.

And now the seventh level soul has matured to the degree that they feel very connected and close to their Guardian Angel. Both are souls in different forms, one 'incarnate' and the other 'discarnate' that have always been intimately connected throughout countless lifetimes. Now the relationship is starting to truly blossom.

Earlier, when the characteristics of Level Five souls were being explained, the distinction between receiving messages from transitioned souls and from Guardian Angels was briefly touched upon. Now we are focusing on Level Seven souls this can be further expanded upon.

All souls, at all levels, have the capability to receive messages from the spiritual realms. In the early stages of our soul's development however, (stages one to four) we tend to tune out these messages because our ego has dominance over our thought patterns and we are therefore less able to tune in to these subtle messages. But all souls at all levels can choose to visit Psychics or Mediums who are able to act on their behalf as the 'message receivers'. So, even an outright spiritual sceptic at Level One could theoretically ask a Medium for a 'message' if they chose to do so. And these messages almost always come from deceased friends, relatives and loved ones. This is because the Medium connects to the spirit realms and tends to automatically connect to those spirits who are intimately connected to the enquirer from the Earth Plane.

But this is a very different scenario from Level Seven souls who have reached a level of spiritual maturity that enables them to connect with their Guardian Angel directly. Most Level Seven souls feel no reason to try and connect with their deceased friends and relatives because they know intuitively that they will be reunited with them at the next transition point. Instead, they are now much more open to receiving messages from their Guardian Angel because these messages are much more important - and relevant - to their current journey. During periods of quiet meditation or internal focusing the Guardian Angels of seventh level souls can communicate quite openly and all seventh level souls are at the right vibrational frequency for seamless connection to occur. As the seventh level soul continues to develop and grow whilst still on the Earth Plane these subtle messages from their Guardian Angel become more frequent and more clear. Help is always at hand for those who have the courage to ask for it.

This feeling of a timeless bond or connection to the spirit world and to their own Guardian Angel and the other spiritual guides is only really achieved and manifested at the seventh level of soul maturity and marks the amazing progress the soul has made on the path. There is now a very strong and eternal intuitive bond between the Earth Plane soul and their Spirit World friends which is a type of love that the earthbound soul may never have experienced with such intensity before. When this has been fully acknowledged the seventh level soul's thoughts are then able to turn towards a new and very important focus.

But this 'new focus' can only start only after the advanced seventh level soul has first found the answers to some deep and searching personal questions:

- Have I learned everything that I should have learned from spirit in this life?
- Have I received everything that I should have received from spirit in this life?
- Have I given everything that spirit wanted me to give in this life?
- Have I taught everything that spirit wanted me to teach in this life?
- Have I truly assimilated the wisdom that spirit wanted me to understand in this life?

Only when the answers to these questions have been answered in total truth and honesty can the seventh level soul start opening his or heart to the next step of their journey and shifting their focus to the next important question.

They will start to think seriously about what needs to be achieved in their *next life* by mentally reviewing all the lessons they have learned during this current incarnation. Only then can they start pondering the next 'big' question on their journey; what new challenges and lessons might await them the 'next time around'?

The Journey of the Fool has come to an end. The quest has been completed and the reward of spiritual wisdom has been granted. The journey is now over and the rewards of enlightenment are waiting. The Fool is no longer a fool but an awakened soul ready to transition to the spiritual realms. The Hero's journey is also over. The third-eye has been opened and visions of eternity, purity and immortality have replaced the earlier egoic 'certainties' built of scepticism, arrogance and ignorance. The Hero's journey on the Earth plane has come to a close. But now a new journey beckons. The journey back to Source. The Soul has completed its ascension from the root to the Crown chakra. The focus now is on connection to Source or divine intelligence, cosmic or unity consciousness, ultimate liberation from body consciousness to spirit consciousness and a liberation from all karmic bonds and debts. Serenity, oneness, bliss and enlightenment are awaiting.

Summary of Stage Seven of the Soul's Path/ Characteristics of a Stage Seven soul

* The ego has finally been fully transcended.
* Following the spiritual path is now the MAIN focus and purpose of life.
* Completing the Soul Contract is now the prime reason for existence and everything else is secondary.
* The soul is starting to look towards the transition into the next life.
* Awareness of karmic law and how to deal with karma.
* Ready to face all life's challenges by totally trusting in the universe.
* A much closer bond with their Guardian Angel and other guides/teachers.

- A closer awareness of 'Source'.
- Hugely sensitive. Will openly cry at world wrongs and injustices.
- Compassion for all without judgement.
- Awareness of other peoples' energies and auras.
- May have acquired 'healing skills'.
- All life is sacred and no living thing must be harmed.
- Sense of 'unity consciousness'.
- A need to be with like-minded/same level souls.
- A need to be immersed in nature - city life no longer tolerable.
- Constant feelings of gratitude and forgiveness.
- Seeking more solitude and silence.
- Less interested in the exterior world and daily news.
- Goes within to find answers.
- Finding it increasingly hard to function on the Earth Plane.
- An aversion to all negative energies.

APPENDIX ONE

Identifying Souls at Different Levels

There are some people who ask me very important questions when I give talks about the stages of the soul. Two of the common questions are about how to identify someone's Stage of soul maturity and how environment, upbringing and genes/DNA relate to the stages of the soul. Both questions are actually very similar so I will cover both topics together.

Firstly, it is never easy to accurately assess which Stage someone is at unless you get to know them quite deeply. It's not simply a matter of observing a stranger for five minutes and then making a biased judgement. Once you fully grasp all the information in this book you will gradually start to develop a natural sort of intuition which will help you to recognise different character traits and behaviour patterns which might give you a clue as to a person's likely level of spiritual maturity. But this can never be more than a rough guess. You are much more likely to know the stage levels of close family members, close friends, long term work colleagues etc. because it takes time to see all the different aspects of their personalities and understand their beliefs, ethics, morals and world views. These are not traits you will glean from observing a complete stranger. Sometimes an error of judgement can create biases in your own mind that may cause you to react in subconsciously inappropriate ways. It is always important to remind yourself that everyone is exactly where they are supposed to be on their path and that is the golden rule.

The good news is that when you do become adept at recognising someone's *likely* level of soul maturity it is also helping you with your own level of maturity and growth. One of the skills we have all been blessed with is to serve those around us by being compassionate and caring. If we are able to assist someone on their path to spiritual wisdom by any action, however insignificant it might seem, that small act of kindness reflects back on us in a positive way enabling our own spiritual growth to flourish.

The second point is about the 'nature versus nurture' debate that has raged for many decades. Many people believe, based on what we have learned in school and from the media, that each of us is the product of our upbringing and our genetic make up. Sociologists and Psychologists love to tell us that we are the end result of what we have been exposed to from birth - in other words the influence of our parents and our peers, the environment we grew up in, our education, our belief systems, our childhood and teenage experiences, our social class etc. This is a huge subject and one that is extremely valid in the context of our soul maturity.

These things DO matter. Our environment, our upbringing and our genetic history all play a major role in making us who we are and developing us as individuals. But, if looked at in isolation, there is a gaping hole in the middle of the entire concept. If we leave "reincarnation" out of the equation - as most 'experts' do, then we are not looking at the whole picture. In short, we are leaving out the most important part!

This is such an important point it needs a little further explanation.

Who we are today - at this very moment - is a combination of various factors. Firstly, we are the product of our generation and we have been shaped by all our life experiences since the day we were born. We have been shaped by the influence of our parents and close family, our school friends, our relations, our teachers, the media and the social and physical environment around us. And we are also, to a degree, shaped by our genetic make-up (although this is not as 'static' as many biologists lead us to believe!). For most academic 'Stage One' souls this is the end of the story - we are the sum of our influences and our biology. Period.

In the spiritual realms though, the story is very different. Yes, it is true that we are shaped by our environment and our genes, but that is only about 5% of the story. In other words these factors only apply in *this particular lifetime*. In the bigger scheme of things, as immortal souls on a spiritual path, we are 95% influenced by the combined subconscious memories from all our previous lives i.e. our karmic/Akashic record.

Although you will never read this in the mainstream media, or academic textbooks, the spiritual world is very clear about this reality. We are, in effect, the sum of all the lives, experiences, challenges, emotions, relationships and beliefs gathered over many millennia. We are the 'walking repository' of everything we have ever learned both good and bad. And this, beyond any other factor, has determined who we are today and what stage of spiritual development we have attained.

APPENDIX TWO

Applying the Wisdom of
the Seven Stages of the Soul

We have now arrived at the end of our journey through this book and it seems pertinent to ask ourselves a very important question - "How can we apply this knowledge about the seven stages of the soul to our current life and how should we use what we have learned in this book to enhance our progress on the path?".

The answer to questions such as these very much depend on our individual responses to everything we have read. Some of us will have felt an emotional and intuitive response to this book whilst others will have a felt a more grounded and academic response. Both responses are equally valid.

In high level terms the book has attempted to answer some of mankind's deepest questions about the reasons for our existence and our place in the universe. Hopefully, most readers will now understand more about their life's purpose and how karma, their previous lives and their progress on their soul path has determined where they are right now - physically and psychologically. This knowledge often provides us with a secure anchor point from which to plan our next steps in life. It is sometimes very hard to make important life decisions if we don't know where we are starting from - so having an idea of where we are standing today on our soul path better enables us to plan ahead. This is crucially important. When we are unable to aim for a precise destination then we remain 'aimless' - and millions of beautiful souls on Earth today still remain essentially aimless whilst continually searching for guidance on their journey.

Knowing where we are on our soul journey and having a clearer insight about which stage of our soul journey we have reached, is extremely empowering for us. It is akin to feeling lost and then being given a detailed map that pinpoints our position so that we know exactly where we are on the map of life. It does not matter whether we are at the start of our journey at Stage One or nearing the end of our journey at Stage Seven. To get from start to finish we still all need to follow the path and on this map there are no short cuts available. But knowing where we are on our own life journey is only part of the goal. The main benefit is that we have now turned a metaphorical key that has opened a door into a treasure trove of wisdom for us. Now we have an insight into everyone else's journey too and this insight is more valuable than gold. Why? Think about it for a moment.

Life is about relationships. Every single person we meet on our life journey has an impact or influence on us. Whether they are strangers, colleagues, family, lovers or enemies every interaction shapes us as individuals and creates our overall concept of what we believe to be our reality. When we have no knowledge about the seven stages of the soul these people are just people. They are just another human being, whether we know a lot about them, or nothing about them, as individuals. They are just faces in the crowd that move in and out of our life with what we believe to be random frequency. Rarely do we perceive them as beautiful, unique, immortal souls meeting their karmic challenges on their own soul paths.

But once we know this truth everything changes because now we are no longer mere participants muddling through a single life on a spinning ball of rock called Earth with millions of others. Instead we are an enlightened soul on a mission to help and serve others on their soul journeys. We have a responsibility. Our wisdom enables us to feel empathy and compassion for *all* souls at whatever stage of maturity they might be at. If we are a Stage Two soul then our goal should be to help as many Stage One souls as we can to make progress on their journey. And if we are a Stage Three soul our goal should be to help as many Stage One and Stage Two souls as we can on their journeys. It is the same all the way through every stage and by the time we reach Stage Seven our mission is to assist *all* our brother and sister souls wherever they may be on their path. That is our mission. Because the more we devote our life to helping others to progress on their path the more spiritual rewards we receive.

There is another huge advantage to understanding the stages of the soul though, which might not at first seem obvious. As we start to use the wisdom imparted in this book we gradually start to think differently about every aspect of our lives. It is as though we have been seeing everyday life through a blurred lens or veil and now that lens or veil has been lifted and we can now see the world with renewed clarity.

When we watch the daily news on TV, read newspapers, go to meetings and social events, attend conferences, witness major events or interact with new acquaintances we no longer think of our fellow human beings as just random 'people'. We now have a deeper insight into who they really are - souls on a journey - and thus a deeper insight into why individuals do the things they do, for good or for bad.

There is an old saying that, "A little knowledge is a dangerous thing" and this is a undoubtedly a true and wise proverb. The corollary might be something like, "Intuitive, spiritual knowledge is a wonderful thing" and it is my belief that this in an equally valid statement. The more we understand our true nature and about who we are and why we are here, the more we can assist our soul brothers and sisters on this magical path we call life.

APPENDIX THREE

Spiritual Crisis in Context

It would be remiss of me not to include, as an Appendix, a few words about a little known topic related to the main themes in this book which may be of additional help to some readers. It will probably come as no surprise to learn that our current health system is ill-equipped to assist anyone with issues relating to their spiritual development and, although quite rare, there are many instances of individuals undergoing natural spiritual growth who occasionally seek medical advice related to unusual feelings or undergoing strange experiences. Transitioning from one soul level to another can bring many new feelings and emotions and if we don't know or understand the cause then we sometimes try to reach out for help and advice.

Although, in most instances, these 'strange feelings' are a perfectly natural by-product of soul development on the Earth Plane, some people turn to health professionals for advice and are usually disappointed by the reaction from an industry that tends to label 'unusual spiritual experiences' as a form of 'psychosis'. In other words a beautiful and natural soul progression is quite likely to be labelled as a 'Mental Health Issue' by some mainstream health professionals. This is not a criticism of the wonderful work our health system undertakes. It is rather, a simple statement of fact that the majority of health professionals are not trained to deal with, or understand, patients or clients who are undergoing, or have already undergone, profound spiritual experiences. And, to be frank, there is a huge difference between being 'ill' and being 'misunderstood'.

Whether the issues might be related to 'Near Death Experiences' (NDE's), 'Out of Body Experiences' (OBE's) or many other types of unexplained experience that might include psychic 'openings', past life memories, encounters with aliens, possession or blissful awakenings etc. our current health system still tends to label such things as a 'Mental Health Issue'.

Fortunately, in recent years, there has been a steadily growing awareness that such experiences should never be assigned to such a vague blanket term as 'Mental Health' - and encouragingly there is increasing recognition that a 'spiritual crisis' is not always the same thing as a mental health issue. An individual undergoing what they perceive to be a spiritual crisis requires specialist help to understand the context of their situation and also help to deal with it in a meaningful and respectful way. Everyone is on a unique spiritual path and essentially this means going through occasional periods of transformation - but transformation is not the same thing as 'psychosis' and should never be treated as such. Anyone going through this crisis or transformation is essentially going through a process that might be temporarily scary or confusing but is ultimately leading them towards spiritual growth or maturity. As one well-respected expert in the field of consciousness research, Stanislav Grof, puts it so eloquently: *"There is a big difference between a spiritual 'emergence' and a spiritual 'emergency'"*.

For more information on this subject, I recommend contacting the "Spiritual Crisis Network" who give excellent support to anyone concerned about their spiritual development: *www.spiritualcrisisnetwork.uk*

AFTERWORD

"There is no other teacher than your own soul".
Swami Vivekananda

We have now arrived at a new beginning.

At the beginning of this book there will have been many unique and beautiful souls seeking the answer to a burning question; "Where am I on my soul journey?". Now that we have learned about each of the seven stages of the soul's journey I hope that question has, to some degree, been answered. Now it is up to you, dear reader, to assimilate this knowledge into your heart intelligence and your soul consciousness and go within to find the internal map and compass that will lead you on the next step of your own wonderful journey.

But before taking your next step on that journey let's remind ourselves of some of the important principles we have learned.

When you fully recognise the power that the ego has had over you throughout your life and you no longer let it control you but simply 'observe' it - and when you surrender yourself to letting the 'universe' guide you instead of your earth-bound desires, a new dimension of consciousness will automatically open up for you. You suddenly become fully supported by 'Source' and by your spirit guides and your every action will then be in alignment with your true mission. When you are fully on track, synchronicity piles on synchronicity and everything falls into place to enable you to achieve your soul's mission more easily. The right people turn up in your life at the right time and you find yourself to be exactly where you are meant to be.

Divine intelligence is guiding you and steering you but without ever compromising your free will. Your sense of personal fulfilment and inner peace increases exponentially because you know, without any shred of doubt, that you are following the right path and learning the right lessons. You know with intuitive certainty that you are *of* the world but not *in* the world because you have now acquired the ability to be the dispassionate observer.

You now comprehend the true meaning of life and you are breathing it and living it. You have now arrived at the point on your soul's journey where everything is in alignment and everything is perfect.

When the right time comes, you will then be ready for life's last, but greatest, adventure - the transition into the next world via the spiritual realms and the return back to Source, where deep peace, unconditional love, true bliss and your devoted Soul Group are waiting to welcome you home.

ABOUT THE AUTHOR

After a successful career as a Senior Executive in the Finance industry Joe then enjoyed a second career as an 'International Management Consultant' working all over the world at Board level in some of the world's leading Companies solving corporate problems throughout the eighties and nineties.

From 2014 - 2018 Joe worked closely with eminent philosopher, scientist and writer Ervin Laszlo as the Managing Director of the 'Laszlo Institute of New Paradigm Research' (L-INPR) in Tuscany, Italy - a conference centre and think-tank which brings together world experts in the fields of holistic and alternative health, consciousness, spirituality, immortality, sustainability and world issues.

In 2016 Joe was invited to join 'Eternea', the US based organisation founded by the 6th man-on-the-moon, Astronaut Edgar Mitchell. Eternea is an organisation focused on research into Consciousness, Reincarnation, Immortality and World Issues.

In 2018 Joe was also appointed UK Director of the "World Sustainable Development Forum" (WSDF-UK) which is focused on meeting the targets of the 'Sustainable Development Goals' (SDG's) and the 'Paris Agreement' on climate change. He also works as an Ambassador for the 'Earth Protectors' organisation.

Joe is an established professional Writer and Conference Speaker with over 3000 articles published to date in leading magazines as well as the author and editor of a number of books. In addition to his work as a Spiritual Mentor he is also a fully qualified Life Coach, Hypnotherapist and Energy Healer.

RECOMMENDED READING

TESTIMONY OF LIGHT
by Helen Greaves

THE HERO WITH A THOUSAND FACES
by Joseph Campbell

JOURNEY OF SOULS
by Michael Newton

DESTINY OF SOULS
by Michael Newton

SAME SOUL, MANY BODIES
by Dr. Brian Weiss

THE ART OF INNER ALCHEMY
by Kelly Schwegel

SCIENCE AND THE
AFTERLIFE EXPERIENCE
by Chris Carter

PROOF OF HEAVEN
by Eben Alexander

LIFE AFTER LIFE
by Ray Moody

MESSAGES OF HOPE
by Suzanne Giesemann

A COMPLETE GUIDE TO THE SOUL
by Patrick Harpur

AUTOBIOGRAPHY OF A YOGI
by Paramahansa Yogananda

LIFE AFTER DEATH
by Deepak Chopra

LIVING DANGEROUSLY
(Osho)

THE INSTRUCTION
by Ainslie MacLeod

LIFE ON THE OTHER SIDE
by Sylvia Browne

SOULS ON EARTH
by Dr. Linda Backman

THE SOUL'S CODE
by James Hillman

JOURNEY OF THE SOUL
by Dr. Brenda Davies

REFERENCED BOOKS

JOURNEY OF THE SOUL
by Dr. Brenda Davies

THE TAROT
by Richard Cavendish

THE HERO WITH A THOUSAND FACES
by Joseph Campbell

WHEELS OF LIFE
by Anodea Judith

THE ART OF INNER ALCHEMY
by Kelly Schwegel

LIVING DANGEROUSLY
(Osho)

THE INSTRUCTION
by Ainslie MacLeod

A NEW EARTH
by Eckhart Tolle

Poem: THE GUEST HOUSE
by Jellaludin Rumi

LIFE ON THE OTHER SIDE
by Sylvia Browne

THE GREAT HUMAN POTENTIAL
by Tom Kenyon and Wendy Kennedy

TESTIMONY OF LIGHT
by Helen Greaves

CREATING THE SOUL BODY
by Robert E. Cox

CPSIA information can be obtained
at www.ICGtesting.com
Printed in the USA
BVHW041522160721
612147BV00015B/1363